A SURVEY OF

# World Cultures

## E U R O P E

Ann Chatterton Klimas

## THE AUTHOR

**Ann Chatterton Klimas** has been involved with education and the preparation of educational materials for the past 20 years. As a teacher and writer, she has worked with students on all levels and written for many different media, including public and commercial broadcasting programs.

A graduate of the Mary Washington College of the University of Virginia, Ann also received a Master of Arts from The Johns Hopkins University.

## PHOTO ACKNOWLEDGMENTS

**Cover Photograph:** Barbara Kondrchek

**Table of Contents:** Eiler Foss

**Chapter 1:** Eiler Foss: open; Greek National Tourist Organization: page 3

**Chapter 2:** Greek National Tourist Organization: open, pages 12, 14, 15, 18; Phyllis Egan: page 20

**Chapter 3:** Italian Government Travel Office: open, pages 29, 36, 38, 39, 40, 41, 42; Mr. and Mrs. Joseph J. Klimas: page 30; Enoch Pratt Free Library Picture Collection: pages 32, 35

**Chapter 4:** British Tourist Authority: open, pages 49, 51, 53; Mr. and Mrs. Joseph J. Klimas: page 55; British Information Services: pages 57, 60, 62

**Chapter 5:** French Government Tourist Office: open, pages 69, 70, 74, 78 (top, right), 79, 80, 83; Food and Wines from France-Inc.: pages 71, 78 (bottom, left); Mr. and Mrs. Joseph J. Klimas: page 77

**Chapter 6:** German Information Center: open, pages 94, 97, 100, 102 (bottom, right), 103, 104, 105; Lufthansa German Airlines: 89, 91, 92; Embassy of the German Democratic Republic: pages 93, 101, 102 (top, left); National Aeronautics and Space Administration: page 98

**Chapter 7:** Polish National Tourist Office: open, pages 111, 112, 115, 119, 120, 124, 125; Susan Biddle-The White House: page 116; *The Catholic Review:* page 123

## STAFF

| | |
|---|---|
| Vice President of Product Development: | Barbara Kondrchek |
| Editor: | T. Sandra Fleming |
| Typesetting: | Lynna Bright |
| Design and Layout: | Gary King |
| Artwork: | Carol Munschauer |
| | Gary King |
| Cover Design: | Norm Myers |

©1990 by Media Materials, Inc.
1821 Portal Street
Baltimore, Maryland 21224.
All rights reserved.

ISBN: 0 - 7916 - 0006 - 8        Order No. 50040

# CONTENTS

# Chapter 3: Italy

# Chapter 4: The United Kingdom

# Chapter 5: France

# Chapter 6: East and West Germany

# Chapter 7: Poland

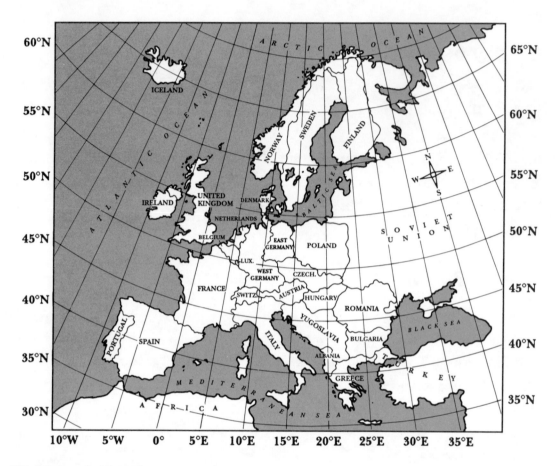

## What Is Culture?

Some people think that *culture* is something fancy. They say that fine art and opera are cultural things.

Fine art and opera are part of culture. But they are not the only parts.

The people who study culture are called *social scientists*. These scientists say that culture involves every part of life. In a way, culture is life. It is the way of life followed by a group of people. It includes art and music. But more importantly, it includes beliefs, customs, inventions, language, technology, and traditions that are shared by a group of people.

**Exploring Culture in This Text**

In this book, you will be looking at the cultural patterns developed by some countries that are in Europe.

Each country you will examine has developed a different set of patterns. These patterns make up an individual culture. Each culture is different from the other.

In this book, you will be looking at several key ideas about the way a culture develops.

- Geography influences culture.
  People often make cultural choices based on the land where they live. For example, farmers can only farm in good soil. They have to live in areas where the soil is fertile.
- Climate influences culture.
  Climate is also a great influence on cultural choices. For example, people that live in warmer climates dress differently and live in different kinds of homes than people who live in colder climates.
- History influences culture.
  A nation's culture can change drastically as a result of historical events. For example, during World War II, over six million Polish people lost their lives. After the war, this loss of lives made it very difficult for Poland to get back on its feet.

You will also look at some key ideas about culture itself, such as:

- Language, literature, and arts reflect culture.
- Inventions reflect culture.

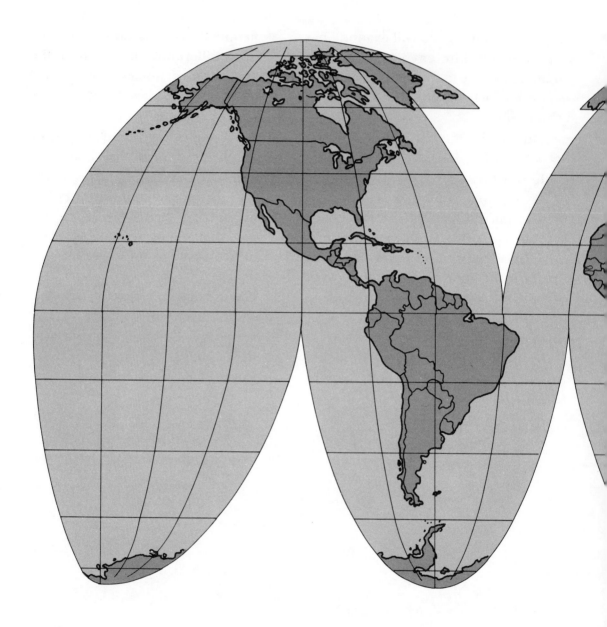

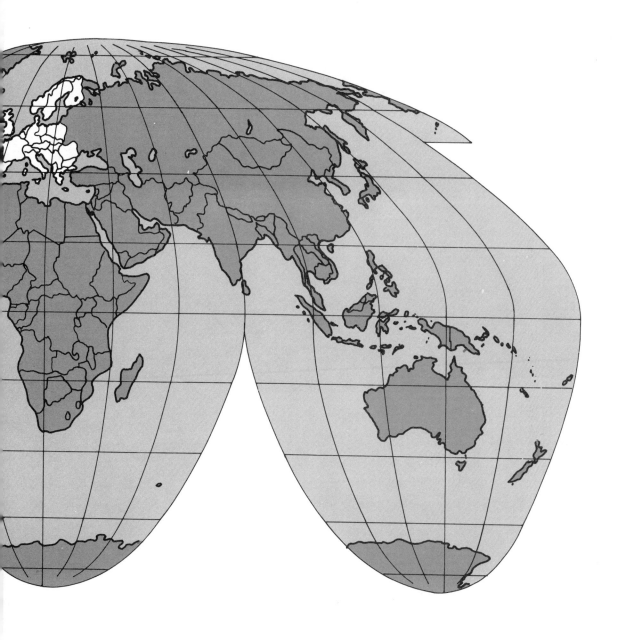

# EUROPE

# EUROPE

**FACTS**

- Europe is made up of 34 separate countries.
- The entire area of Europe is about 4,063,000 square miles.
- Europe is the second most populated continent in the world.
- About 50 languages and over 100 dialects are spoken in Europe.
- In most European countries, over 90% of the people are literate.

## PART 1:
### The European Continent

Europe is the second smallest *continent* in the world. A continent is a large land division. Only Australia is smaller. However, Europe has a large population. About one-seventh of all the people on Earth live in Europe.

Europe stretches from the Atlantic Ocean on the west to the western part of the Soviet Union in the east. The eastern part of the Soviet Union is part of Asia. Europe's northern border is the Arctic Ocean. Its southern border is the Mediterranean Sea. Europe is actually a part of a large land mass. It occupies one-fifth of that land. The other four-fifths are part of another continent. That continent is called Asia.

**There Are 34 Countries in Europe**

There are 34 separate countries in Europe. Generally, these countries are small. The five smallest ones

# EUROPE

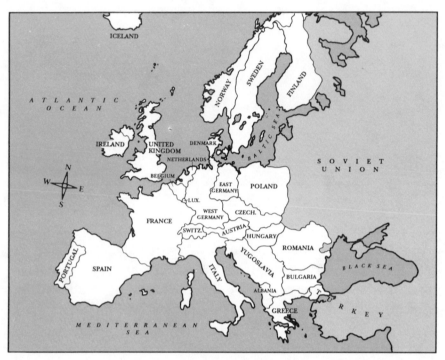

**Map Study:** *List two countries that border on the Mediterranean Sea. Name two countries that border on the Atlantic Ocean. Which country is farther south: Italy or Sweden? Which country is farther north: Finland or Spain? Is France in Eastern or Western Europe?*

could all fit within the city limits of Phoenix, Arizona. The entire area of Europe is not much larger than that of the United States. Two large countries in Europe are the European part of the Soviet Union and France. European Russia has an area of over two million square miles.

**REVIEW**

**Directions:**
Number your paper from 1 to 5. Answer the following questions.
1. What is the smallest continent in the world?
2. What is Europe's northern border?
3. What other continent shares the same land mass as Europe?
4. How many countries are there in Europe?
5. What European country has an area of over two million square miles?

## PART 2:
## European Culture

European culture began thousands of years ago. During this ancient time, many tribes roamed throughout the continent. They settled in different areas and met and mixed with other groups. Many Europeans can trace their roots directly back to these ancient tribes. Their culture started there.

Over time, these cultures grew and changed. Nations were formed. The idea of a national culture grew. A national culture is the culture of a group of people living within certain political borders.

In some parts of Europe, national cultures have started to think of themselves in a new way. They have started to think about themselves as Europeans. This is particularly true in Western Europe. Twelve countries there have formed an economic group called the *European Economic Community*, or EEC. They have united to help each others' economy.

### European Cultures Are
### Different From Each Other

There is not one European culture. The cultures that developed in each area are unique. They are vastly different from each other. Their languages are different. Their values are different. Their governments are different.

The Europeans like this diversity. Individual countries have spent a great deal of time and money to preserve their own cultures. The cultural differences we see actually make up the national character of each nation.

*Greece was one of the first major cultures in Europe.*

# SPOTLIGHT
## S T O R Y

## How Europe Got Its Name

**E**urope was named after a Greek goddess. In ancient Greece, many people believed in a system of gods and goddesses. The Greeks made up many stories and legends about these figures. They used these stories to explain some of the things about their world that they did not understand.

One of the goddesses was named Europa. She was very beautiful. One night, Europa had a very puzzling dream. She dreamt that two continents were fighting over her. The continents took the shape of women. One of the continents was Asia.

The dream puzzled Europa. She asked her friends to meet her in a nearby meadow. The meadow was by the sea. Her friends all came to help her.

Zeus looked down on the girls as they talked. At that moment, Cupid shot an arrow into Zeus' heart. Immediately, Zeus fell in love with Europa.

Zeus changed himself into a beautiful white bull. He appeared to the girls. He was so gentle that no one was afraid of him. Europa was fascinated. The bull lay down before her. Europa quickly sat on his back. She told the others to do the same.

Before anyone else could move, the bull swam away. Europa realized then that he must be a god. Zeus brought Europa to Crete. The two married. A new civilization began.

**Stop and Review**

Write the answers to these questions on your paper.

1. Why did the ancient Greeks make up stories about gods and goddesses?
2. Why did Europa ask her friends to meet her in a meadow?
3. What happened that made the god Zeus fall in love with Europa?
4. In what form did Zeus first appear to Europa?
5. When did Europa realize that she was being carried off by a god?

*Zeus, in the form of a beautiful white bull, carries off Europa.*

## There Are Many Areas Where Cultural Differences Can Be Seen

Government is one area where the differences in European cultures can be seen. Since World War II, many countries in Eastern Europe have adopted *Communist* governments. This has set up a division in Europe. Most Western European nations are not Communist. In general, governments in Communist countries allow their citizens less personal freedom than non-Communist countries.

Another area where there are cultural differences is between people that live in the cities and people that live in the country. People who live in the great cities of Europe usually have a higher *standard of living* than people who live in rural areas.

## European Cultures Have Some Common Attitudes

All European cultures do have some ideas that they share. Most believe that their families are very important. A majority of Europeans are quite aware of their place in society. There has always been a division between the noble, or ruling classes and the working classes. Europeans also share the belief that their governments should provide many services for them. The government usually controls television and radio stations. Some European governments also pay for their citizens' medical care.

As a group, Europeans are also some of the most well-educated people in the world. In most European countries, over 90 percent of the people can read and write.

Most Europeans also take great pride in their past. Their continent has been called the birthplace of Western civilization. The history and culture of their continent has greatly shaped the history and culture of many other continents.

---

R
E
V
I
E
W

**Directions:**
Number your paper from 1 to 5. Answer the following questions.
1. How did most European cultures first start?
2. What is the EEC?
3. What is one major difference between European cultures?
4. In your opinion, what is one advantage of having so many different cultures in Europe?
5. What are three basic areas where we can see similar ideas in different European cultures?

# MAP SKILLS

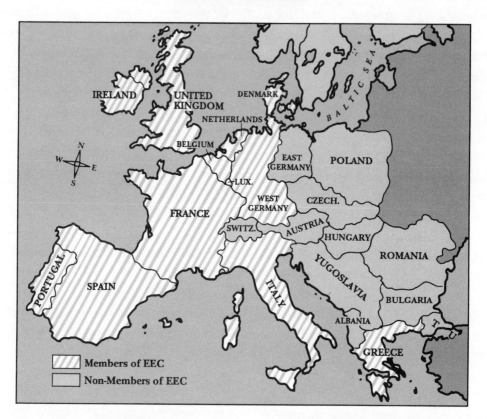

# THE EUROPEAN ECONOMIC COMMUNITY

The European Economic Community (EEC) is an economic organization made up of 12 Western European countries that have joined together to help each other's economies. Usually, nations put a special tax on goods coming into their country from another. Countries in the EEC do not do this if the goods come from another EEC country. Workers from EEC countries do not have to get special permission to work in another EEC country. The EEC has a government that makes decisions about the group's policies. All member countries have a say in this government. It includes a Council of Ministers and a European Parliament.

**Directions:**

Number your paper from 1 to 6. Answer the questions using the information given on the map and the key.

1. Is Poland a member of the EEC?
2. Is East Germany a member of the EEC?
3. Is Switzerland a member of the EEC?
4. Is West Germany a member of the EEC?
5. Which country belonging to the EEC is located the farthest west?
6. Which EEC member is farthest east?

# CHAPTER 1 REVIEW

## Summary of Introduction

*Culture includes beliefs, customs, inventions, language, technology, and traditions shared by a group of people. Geography, climate, and history influence the cultural choices a group makes. Language, literature, the arts, and inventions reflect the choices a culture has made.*

*Europe is the second smallest continent in the world. There are 34 independent countries in Europe.*

*Europe has many cultures. Most of them began thousands of years ago. Each national culture is unique. Some major cultural differences can be seen in the division of Communist and non-Communist nations. There is also a great difference between life in European cities and in rural areas.*

*European cultures have some common attitudes. These similarities can be seen in family life, social class, and government. Most Europeans are well-educated and very proud of their past.*

## Critical Thinking Skills

**Directions:** Give some serious thought to the questions below. Be sure to answer in complete sentences.

1.  How would you define culture?
2.  Name three of the factors that can influence cultural choices. Give an example of a cultural choice that is made because of one of these factors.
3.  Name a tradition that is part of your own culture. Explain how it differs from another culture.
4.  Do you think cultures in the United States share the Europeans' concern about social class? Defend your position.
5.  Why do you think so many people in Europe know how to read and write?

## For Discussion

**Directions:** Discuss these questions with your class. Appoint one member of the class to write the ideas you discover on the board.

1.  Europeans generally believe that their family is very important to them. Do you think most people in America feel the same way?
2.  Why does knowing and speaking the same language help people get along with each other?
3.  Some of the smaller countries in Europe are no larger than the average American city. What are some of the advantages and disadvantages of being so small?
4.  What recent events in your culture have influenced the way you live?

## Write It!

**Directions:** Your family is a subculture. It is part of the American culture. Write a letter to a pen pal in a European country. Explain the way your family celebrates birthdays. This is a cultural trait that changes from culture to culture.

## For You to Do

**Directions:** Each member of your class has a unique cultural background. Make a chart that lists all members of the class. After each name, write the cultures from which each person came. For example, someone in your class many have had parents that came from the Japanese culture, or grandparents that were born in Jamaica. Compare the information you discover. Which culture appears most frequently on the chart? Which culture appears the least? Are any of the cultures listed from Europe?

# GREECE

- Greece's mainland is on the southern tip of the Balkan Peninsula.
- No part of Greece is more than 85 miles from the sea.
- The capital of Greece is Athens.
- About 40 percent of Greek workers are farmers.
- Rural areas in Greece preserve many older traditions of their culture.

## PART 1:
## Geography and Climate of Greece

**G**reece's mainland is located on the tip of the Balkan Peninsula. A *peninsula* is a land form that is surrounded by water on three sides. The Greek peninsula is also divided by many large bodies of water. The Gulf of Corinth almost cuts it in two.

This closeness to the sea has always played a great part in Greek culture. Since ancient times, the Greeks have been good sailors. The sea was their route to other parts of the known world. They explored and settled in the places they found. Greeks also traded goods and shared their culture with others. In recent times, Greeks have owned large fleets of ships that carry goods all over the world.

The Greeks have always been fishermen. Fish of all kinds are a large part of the Greek diet.

# GREECE

**Map Study:** *Greece is a nation of many islands. Is Mikonos (Mykonos) an island? Is Olympia an island or a city? What nation is the island of Rhodes near? Are there more islands in the Aegean or Ionian Sea? What is the name of the sea near the island of Crete? Is Sparti (Sparta) on the mainland of Greece or on the island of Patmos? What nation is the island of Kerkira (Corfu) near?*

## Greece Has Many Islands

Greece also includes 437 islands. An *island* is a landform that is surrounded by water on all sides. These islands make up about 20 percent of Greece's land area. People live on about one-half of these islands.

The largest Greek island is Crete. It is 60 miles south of the Greek mainland. The Minoan culture developed on Crete. In ancient times, Greeks believed that Zeus was born here. Zeus was the most important god in their religion.

Two of the other large islands are Rhodes and Corfu. Corfu is also called Kerkira. This island has been a resort area for many centuries.

## Greece Is Very Mountainous

Mountains and the hills that surround them cover almost 70 percent of Greece. The mountains cut the country into many small regions. Traveling from one area to another is very difficult.

This separation has influenced Greek culture. Each village developed its own language. The languages were somewhat alike. These forms of the same language are called *dialects*. Each village also developed many other traditions and beliefs that were unique to its own people.

## Greece Has Very Poor Soil

Some Greeks tell an interesting story about the way their country was formed. They say that when God was making the Earth, He sifted the soil through a strainer. He gave each country a part of the good, rock-free soil. Then, he threw away the rocks. They all landed in Greece.

The rocky soil has made it difficult for Greece's farmers. They have to work very hard to grow crops in such poor soil. Only the few valleys in Greece have land that is more fertile.

## Greece Is the Closest European Nation to the Equator

The *equator* is an imaginary line that circles the Earth at its middle. Countries that are close to the equator have the warmest climates of any region on Earth.

Greece is the most southern European nation. It is close to the equator. Therefore, Greece has a very warm climate.

Greeks like their warm weather and take full advantage of it. Often, they meet in open air cafés to talk. Their homes are generally small, because they can actually live outside during most of the year.

## Greece Has Rainy Winters

Greece gets most of its rain during the winter months. Rainfall is heaviest in the northwest and decreases as you move southeast.

This weather pattern affects Greek life. In the summer, it rarely rains. In *rural* areas, some people get their water from wells. In the summer, these wells often dry up and the people have to get water from other places. Sometimes, they have to carry the water by hand.

In the winter, the rain makes the water in the rivers very high. In the summer, the rivers usually dry up.

---

**R E V I E W**

**Directions:**
Number your paper from 1 to 5. Answer the following questions.
1. Write a complete definition of *island*. How is an island different from a peninsula?
2. How has Greece's closeness to the sea affected Greek culture?
3. What geographic form makes it difficult to travel in Greece?
4. How would you describe Greece's climate?
5. How has Greece's climate influenced Greek culture?

## PART 2:
## History of Greece

We know that Greek cultures developed many thousands of years ago. There were two very important early cultures.

One developed on the island of Crete. It first came into being about 3000 B.C. This culture is called the *Minoan culture.* It was named after one of the culture's great kings, King Minos. The Minoans had a very complex culture that prized art and loved beautiful things. They traded the goods they made with people in Egypt.

During this time, another important culture developed. It was called the *Mycenaean culture.* This culture developed on the Greek mainland.

*Visitors to Knossos can still see the ruins of King Minos' palace. It was built hundreds of years before the birth of Christ.*

Some people also call this culture the *Helladic civilization,* because the Greek mainland is sometimes called *Hellas.*

The Mycenaean culture was very advanced. These early Greeks were also great soldiers because they often had to defend their land from invaders.

**The City-State**

The Minoan and Mycenaean cultures disappeared by about 1100 B.C. Soon, other groups began to take their place.

These groups were called *city-states.* The Greeks called these units a *polis.* These city-states were very small. Some had less people than a modern high school. But each city-state was completely independent from the others. The only time the city-states united was to fight. Together, they defeated the Persians that invaded their land.

There were two great city-states: Athens and Sparta. Both had a great deal of power.

Athens had a powerful army and navy. Other city-states joined with Athens in time of war for their own protection.

## The Acropolis

We have come to think of the Acropolis as one special place. It is a high hill in the center of Athens. Today, it contains the ruins of many ancient Greek buildings.

However, each city-state, or polis, usually had an acropolis. *Acropolis* meant "high city." The acropolis in each city-state was a high, rocky hill, around which the city built a wall of rocks. This was their way of protecting the polis from attack. From the Acropolis, people could roll boulders down on their enemies.

Today, the Acropolis in Athens is at the center of town. It is about 200 feet above the rest of the city. Many religious temples were built on this hill. In ancient times, this made it easier for the Greeks to protect these sacred places. The ruins of these temples are still standing today.

The chief temple honors Athena. It is called the Parthenon. Athena was a Greek goddess. Athens was named after her. The Greeks prayed to her so that she would protect the city.

Two other temples are located on the Acropolis. They both honor Athena. One is called the Erechtheum. It is known for the beautiful statues of maidens that support one of its porches. The other temple is the Temple of Nike Athena. *Nike* means "bringer of peace" in Greek. This temple shows a three-dimensional picture of the Greeks defeating the Persians.

Athens was one of the first city-states to have a democratic form of government. Each male citizen had to take part in an assembly that made the laws. The assembly was held once every nine days. There, the men made all the important decisions for the government. This is called direct democracy.

Sparta hated and feared Athens. This city-state did not have a democratic form of government. In fact, Sparta was like a huge military base. All Spartan men were full-time soldiers. The young boys in Sparta lived in military barracks where they trained to be soldiers.

The government controlled every part of a Spartan's life. It tried to keep people from reading so they would not learn new ideas.

The differences between Athens and Sparta made them rivals. They both wanted to lead the other city-states. Eventually, the two went to war against each other and Sparta defeated Athens.

### Greece Becomes Part of Macedonia

Despite its early greatness, Greece did not really become a united country until 338 B.C. Philip II of Macedonia had conquered many of the Greek city-states. He organized them into a great empire. His son, Alexander the Great, conquered more lands. Both Philip and Alexander admired the Greek culture.

They spread its language and customs to other lands.

## Greece Becomes Part of Other Empires

When Alexander died, there was no leader to take his place. The Roman Empire easily conquered the weakened Greeks. By 146 B.C., all of Greece became a province of Rome.

*These Greek soldiers belong to a special corps called euzones. They guard the Tomb of the Unknown Soldier in Athens.*

In turn, the Greeks were taken into other *empires*. In 395 A.D., the Byzantine Empire split apart from Rome. Greece was part of this empire for over 1,000 years. By 1453, the Ottoman Empire had taken over all parts of the Byzantine Empire. Greece became part of the Ottoman Empire for over 300 years.

Greek governments had disappeared. But Greek culture never did. Many of the conquerors adapted Greek ways.

## Greece Rebels

By the 1800s, many Greeks wanted their country to be free. Greek soldiers began fighting in 1821. They were outnumbered by the Turkish army. But the Greeks finally drove out their invaders. In 1829, Greece became an independent country once again. France, Great Britain, and Russia were the first to recognize Greece as an independent nation.

## Greece During the World Wars

In June of 1917, Greece entered World War I on the side of the *Allies*: France, Great Britain, Russia, the United States, and many others. The peace treaties that followed the war gave Greece additional territories, including Thrace and some islands in the Aegean Sea.

When World War II started, Greece tried to remain neutral. However, in 1940, Italy attacked Greece. German soldiers soon followed. In a few short months, they had occupied the entire Greek nation. Greeks suffered greatly under

German occupation. Some decided to fight back by joining secret resistance groups. Toward the end of the war, Germany started to withdraw its soldiers. Soon, troops from the United Kingdom joined Greek resistance members to regain control of Greece.

### Greece in Modern Times

Independence has not been easy for Greece. The country has had many forms of government. Originally, a king was appointed to lead the country, but many Greeks did not like this. They wanted the people to play a part in their own government. They wanted a *republic.* Greece has had many *constitutions.* Some said the king had all power in government. Others supported a republic. Today,

*This is the building in Athens where the Greek Parliament meets. It used to be the home of Greece's royal family. The Greek Parliament has 300 members. All members are elected to four-year terms.*

Greece has a republican form of government.

These political problems have had a strong effect on the country. Greece is no longer the world leader that it was in ancient times.

REVIEW

**Directions:**
Number your paper from 1 to 5. Answer the following questions.
1. What were the names of the two oldest Greek cultures?
2. How would you define a city-state?
3. What were two of the empires that conquered Greece?
4. How did Greece regain its independence?
5. How have political problems affected Greece in modern times?

# GREECE

## PART 3:
## Language, the Arts, and Inventions

People were speaking forms of the Greek language thousands of years ago. Scientists have found evidence of this. In 1953, a cryptographer (someone who studies codes) proved that people were speaking Greek as early as 1400 B.C. He translated some writings that were made at the time of the Mycenaean culture. Greek is one of the oldest languages that are still spoken.

### The Greeks Had Many Dialects

We have learned that Greek villages are very isolated. The mountains in Greece make travel difficult. The separated villages each developed their own form of Greek. These forms were called dialects. These dialects were similar enough that Greeks from one region could understand Greeks from another.

In ancient times, there were four main divisions of these dialects. One was the language of Athens, called *Attic*. Attic became the standard language for writers and leaders.

Alexander the Great spread this language throughout the lands he conquered. Soon many people in his empire spoke *koine*. Koine is a simplified form of Attic. The New Testament is written in koine.

### The Greek Alphabet

Almost all European alphabets are based on the original alphabet used in Greece. The word *alphabet* comes from the first two letters of the Greek alphabet: alpha and beta.

| Capital letter | A | B | Γ | Δ | E | Z | H | Θ | I | K | Λ | M | N | Ξ | O | Π | P | Σ | T | Y | Φ | X | Ψ | Ω |
|---|---|---|---|---|---|---|---|---|---|---|---|---|---|---|---|---|---|---|---|---|---|---|---|---|
| Small letter | α | β | γ | δ | ε | ζ | η | θ | ι | κ | λ | μ | ν | ξ | o | π | ρ | σ | τ | υ | φ | χ | ψ | ω |
| Name of letters | alpha | beta | gamma | delta | epsilon | zeta | eta | theta | iota | kappa | lambda | mu | nu | xi | omikron | pi | rho | sigma | tau | upsilon | phi | khi | psi | omega |
| Equivalent "Roman" letter | A / a | B / b | G / g | D / d | E (short) / e | Z / z | E (long) / e | Th / th | I / i | K / k | L / l | M / m | N / n | X / x | O (short) / o | P / p | R / r | S / s | T / t | U / u | Ph,F / ph,f | Kh,Ch / kh,ch | Ps / ps | O (long) / o |

*The Greek alphabet has 24 letters. The corresponding letters from our own Roman alphabet are listed below them.*

| Some Greek Words | | |
| --- | --- | --- |
| **English** | **Greek** | **Pronunciation** |
| Good night | Kalinikta | Kah-lee-nik´-tah |
| Please | Parakalo | Pah-rah-kah-low´ |
| Yes | Ne | Neh |
| Thank you | Efkaristo | Ef-kah-ree-sto´ |

The Greeks adapted their alphabet from another alphabet. It was the one used by the Phoenicians. In turn, the Greeks gave their language to other nations. The Romans took the Greek letters and changed them. The English language adopted the Roman letters. Many other languages followed this same path.

## Modern Greek

The language Greeks speak today began to take shape around the year 900 A.D. Greece itself was absorbed into the Byzantine and Ottoman Empires. But its people never stopped speaking Greek. Today, about nine million people speak Greek.

There are two forms of modern Greek. The *demotic* form is the language that the people speak. It is also the language in which most Greek books are written. The other form of Greek is called *katharevousa*. It is the language used in government documents. Most scientific books are also written in this form of Greek.

## Some Greek Words

Many languages have adapted Greek words into their language. Many of these words have to do with the Greek inventions that they named. For example, the Greeks invented a form of government they called demokratia. We call it democracy. Greek scholars developed the science of thinking. Today, we call that science *philosophy*. This comes from two Greek words. It means "love of knowledge or learning."

Look at the chart above. It contains some words that are used in Greece today. The words are written using our own alphabet.

## Ancient Greece Gave the World Literature

Greek culture was the first to use many forms of literature. Their *epic*

# SPOTLIGHT
## S T O R Y

## Greek Drama

The citizens of Athens were the first to enjoy Greek plays. Dramas and comedies were first created during Athens' Golden Age.

The plays themselves were held outside. The Athenians built special outdoor theaters that were often carved into the sides of hills. People sat in seats that ringed a central dancing circle. Thousands attended these plays. We know this because some of these theaters still exist today. Many had seats for 10,000 people.

*Greeks came to theatres like this one for all-day performances of several plays. If they enjoyed a play, they whistled and stomped their feet. If they didn't, they booed and threw stones at the actors.*

At the center of the seats was a ring where the actors performed, called the orchestra. Behind the orchestra, there was a skene. This was a building that served as the background for the play. The actors moved behind the skene when the plays called for any violence. Athenian playgoers never saw any murders on stage.

The actors that performed were all males. There were never more than three actors in a play. They played many different parts, including those of the women in the plays. The actors wore masks that were much larger than their faces. They changed masks as they changed characters. The actors also wore decorated shoes and giant headdresses. These made the actors appear to be much taller than they really were, and allowed spectators sitting far away to be able to see them.

Athenians prized and enjoyed their theaters. They became the first formal stages in the world.

### Stop and Review

Write the answers to these questions on your paper.

1. In what city-state were the first Greek plays performed?
2. How were the theaters in ancient Greece different than the theaters we have now?
3. What is a skene? How was it used?
4. How many actors usually performed in an ancient Greek play? How many actresses were there?
5. Why did the actors wear large masks and giant headdresses?

*poems* were the first ever recorded. Many later cultures used this form to retell their own early history. Greeks also created the *lyric poem*. Lyric poems relate the feelings of the poet.

The Greeks also created two important forms of drama: tragedy and comedy.

Greek writers also recorded the history of their times. Scholars today still use these histories to study the culture of the ancient world.

### Greek Literature Today

Early Greek writers were pioneers. They introduced many new kinds of literature. They were part of a strong, artistic culture.

When Greece became part of other empires, its writers had a different job. They had to work to preserve Greek culture. They mostly wrote folk stories. This trend continued until this century.

Slowly, Greek authors have started to explore new ground. Powerful novelists such as Nikos Kazantzakis began writing books like *Zorba the Greek* and *The Last Temptation of Christ.* In 1963, George Seferis received a Nobel prize for his lyric poems. This was the first time a Greek had been awarded this important literary prize.

### Inventions

Early Greek thinkers observed the patterns they saw in nature. They discovered the principles of mathematics that we still use to study mathematics today. They discovered many laws of astronomy. The ancient Greeks even invented a new science called philosophy. Philosophy is the study of learning and thinking. The word philosophy is a Greek word. It means "love of learning."

The Greeks also invented many practical things to help them. The first person to ever draw a map was Greek. A Greek called Archimedes invented a way to get water up from deep wells, called the water screw. This device is still used today to irrigate farmland.

---

**R E V I E W**

**Directions:**
Number your paper from 1 to 5. Answer the follwing questions.
1. What is koine? How did people in other parts of the world learn it?
2. Where does the word *alphabet* come from?
3. Which form of modern Greek do people speak in everyday life?
4. What two forms of drama did the early Greeks invent?
5. Name two Greek inventions that are still being used today.

## PART 4:
## Life in Modern Greece

Greece's money system is based on the *drachma*. In 1989, there averaged about 160 drachma to the American dollar. The Greeks also use a *lepta*. One hundred lepta equal one drachma.

About 40 percent of Greek workers are farmers. Their farms are very small. There is not much flat land in Greece, and most of the soil is poor. Greek farmers have to work hard to make their farms profitable. Some of the crops they grow are lemons, olives, and grapes. The Greeks do not raise a lot of cattle. They buy most of their meat and dairy products from other countries.

Recently, Greece has tried to build up its industry. However, this

*Most of the soil in Greece is very dry and rocky. This can make farming rather difficult.*

effort has been difficult. The Greek economy was almost destroyed during World War II. It has taken the Greeks a long time to recover.

**The Family**

Family life is very important in Greece. Traditional Greek values are a large part of family living. This is particularly true in rural areas of the country.

Greek parents prize their children. If you visit a Greek family, you are expected to bring a special gift for the children. In return, the children have a great deal of respect for their parents and older relatives.

Traditionally, parents have a great deal of control over their children. They usually make all the important decisions for them, including choosing or approving of who they will marry. Some Greek parents make sure their daughters have a *dowry*. This is a sum of money or property that wives give to their husbands when they marry. In many cases, the sons in a family cannot marry until their sisters have. By tradition, the oldest daughter in a Greek family must be the first to marry. Her younger sisters will also marry in the order of their ages.

Although Greek women have the same rights as Greek men according to law, this is not always the case in reality. For example, most women do not take an active part in politics.

Since the mid-1900s, these traditional values have been changing, particularly in the cities. As people have become more educated and more independent, they do not depend on their families as much as they have in the past.

## Education

Greek students must attend school from ages 6 through 11. The Greek government pays for this education. However, some students do attend private schools where their parents pay for their *tuition*. Most Greek students wear uniforms that are usually blue and white. These are the national colors of Greece and the colors of the Greek flag.

Greek students attend primary school for six years. Then they go to a secondary school, or high school, for another six years. If they want to continue to a college or university, they must pass special examinations. It is not easy to pass these tests. Today, there are about 20 universi-

ties and colleges in Greece. There are also several technical institutes, where people can prepare for many different careers.

In general, the modern Greek education system has been successful. It has reduced the number of citizens who cannot read and write. People who cannot read or write are called *illiterate*. About 12 percent of Greeks today are illiterate.

## Dancing

Greeks love to dance. Each region has its own special dances. Greek men often dance together in a group, or sometimes they dance alone. They dance to the music of the *bouzouki*, a type of mandolin.

The people who watch the dancers often become very excited. Sometimes they throw plates on the floor. This is the Greek way of saying they are having a good time.

## Sports

Greeks also love sports. As in most European countries, soccer is very popular.

No place in Greece is very far from the sea. Water sports, such as swimming and diving, are very popular. During the summer, many Greek families rent houses close to the sea.

# GREECE

## The Kafenion

Greek life revolves around the local café. The Greeks call it a *kafenion*. In the city, both men and women go to the kafenion. In rural areas, the kafenions are strictly for men.

These coffee houses are often outdoors in a central part of the town. People in the kafenion usually order a cup of coffee. It is very thick and strong, and is served in a small cup. The waiter will also bring a glass of water with each cup of coffee. People at the kafenion sip coffee and watch what is going on around them. They talk about events of the day, politics, or sports.

## Festivals and Religion

There are many festivals in Greece. Sometimes, a city celebrates its own special day. Other times, the festivals celebrate the gathering of a new crop. Often, the festivals are religious.

Greeks hold their religion very dear. Almost 98 percent of them belong to the Greek Orthodox Church. Greek law says that Greeks have freedom of religion. They can follow any faith. However, most Greeks think that the only true Greek is one who belongs to the Greek Orthodox Church. The Greek government supports the church, and children are taught the beliefs of this religion at home and in their schools.

The most important religious festival of the year takes place around Easter. Lent is a period in the Greek religious calendar forty days before Easter. Before Lent begins, the Greeks celebrate for an entire month with parades and festivals. The first day of Lent is called Clean Monday. People go to the country for picnics. Many fly kites.

During the week before Easter, Greeks go to church services every night. On the Saturday before Easter, they bring candles to church. Before midnight, they blow out their candles. The priest brings in a new candle and lights a worshippers' candle. The light is passed around until all the candles glow. The people carry the candles home and eat a special breakfast. When daylight comes, they start cooking the Easter lamb.

All through the day people greet each other by saying, "Khristos anesti." It means "Christ is risen."

## Eating

The Greeks have developed a type of cooking that is very much their own. Greek cooks take advantage of the crops that grow well in their country. Olives are one of these. The Greeks squeeze the olives to get their oil. They use olive oil to cook everything, even fried eggs.

Greeks do not eat much meat. Most beef has to be imported into their country and it is very expensive. However, the Greeks do enjoy lamb. Greek families will often prepare a roast lamb when they want to celebrate a special occasion.

Greek cooking also uses a great deal of seafood. The Greeks have always farmed the seas. Today, Greeks enjoy eating a wide variety of seafood, including squid and octopus.

Many Greek dishes are now popular all over the world. Perhaps you have already sampled some. If you live in an urban area where there are people of Greek ancestry, chances are you can find many Greek specialties at the corner sub shop. Some Greek foods that may sound familiar are gyro (grilled lamb, served on pita bread), souvlakia (lamb and vegetables, grilled on a skewer), feta (cheese made from goat's milk), spanakopita (spinach and feta in a thin pastry-like shell), and baklava (pastry made with honey and almonds). Other Greek delicacies include dolmades (grape leaves stuffed with rice), keftedes (meatballs), kalamarakia (squid), and moussaka (a casserole of eggplant and ground lamb). Which of these Greek dishes would you like to try?

Most Greeks eat their main meal of the day at night. Dinner is served between 8:00 and 9:00 P.M. The oldest person at the table is always served first. People use their fingers to pick up and eat some Greek dishes. Bread is served with every meal. But the Greeks place it directly on the table. They do not use a separate bread plate.

**R E V I E W**

**Directions:**
Number your paper from 1 to 5 and answer the following questions.
1. What is the basic coin in the Greek money system?
2. How do many Greeks make their living?
3. Describe one tradition of the Greek cultural pattern of marriage.
4. To what religion do most Greeks belong?
5. If you wanted to prepare a traditional Greek meal, what would you serve your guests?

## MAP SKILLS

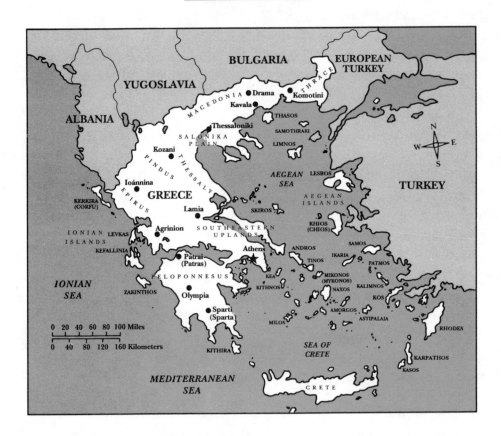

## USING PARTS OF A MAP

A map is a representation of a piece of land. It can show many different kinds of information. For example, a political map shows the towns, cities, or regions that exist in a specific area. The legend, or key, of a map helps you understand the information that it gives. The legend shows the scale of the map. The scale is the unit of measurement used on the map to show actual distances. It also shows you what symbols the map uses for things such as roads and capital cities. Most maps are drawn so that the northern direction is at the top of the map.

This is shown by a drawing of a compass some place on the map.

**Directions:** Answer the questions below, using the information given on the map.

1. What is the capital city of Greece?
2. What is the scale this map uses? Using this scale, approximately how far is it from Athens to the island of Crete?
3. Which countries are on the northern border of the Greek mainland?
4. Which kind of information does this map give? What kind of a map is it?

# CHAPTER 2 REVIEW

## Summary of Greece

*Greek culture has long been tied to the sea. Its mainland is a peninsula and its many islands extend this nation's borders to the Ionian and Aegean Seas. Farmers in this nation, which is near the equator, have had to deal with very poor soil and a warm climate.*

*Greek culture started centuries ago, with the Minoan and Mycenaean cultures, and grew to importance under Philip of Macedonia. Greece also became part of the Roman, Byzantine, and Ottoman Empires. These cultures shared many of the traditional parts of Greek culture.*

*Greece has made many significant contributions to literature, drama, science, philosophy, and mathematics. The Greeks today speak a form of one of the oldest languages known. They continue to farm the land of their ancestors, holding dear the ways of their cultural past. Their family, their love of their country, and the resources of their land are an important part of modern Greek culture.*

## Critical Thinking Skills

**Directions:** Give some serious thought to the questions below. Be sure to answer in complete sentences.

1. What features of Greek geography make it hard for Greek farmers to grow their crops?
2. If you were an ancient Greek, would you prefer to live in Athens or Sparta? Give at least two reasons for your decision.
3. In your opinion, why has Greece not been as important in modern times as it has been in the past?
4. Most scholars say that Greece is the cradle of Western civilization. What does this mean? Do you feel this is true?

## For Discussion

**Directions:** Discuss these questions with your class. Appoint one member of the class to write the ideas you discover on the board.

1. What are some of the features that you would expect to find in the homes in such a warm climate as Greece has? For example, would there be large windows? Screen doors? Patios? How would these homes differ from homes in colder areas of the world such as northern Canada?
2. After the fall of the Greek and Roman civilizations, many artistic and cultural traditions were lost. During the Renaissance, they were rediscovered. How would the world have been different if the traditions and artistry of ancient Greek cultures had not been lost?
3. The New Testament was written in koine. What does this tell you about this early Greek language?

## Write It!

**Directions:** Pretend that your parents are Greek. You have to write a special column for your school newspaper. You want to write about Greek culture. Your article can only be 50 words long. Write it!

## For You to Do

**Directions:** Divide your class into teams of three or four. Using these Greek root words and a dictionary, find as many words as you can that have these word parts in them. Compare your lists.

Root Words:

| demo- | hypno- | -sophy | cosmo- |
| -cracy | psycho- | -politan | -graphy |

# ITALY

> F •  Italy is in southern Europe.
> A •  Italy borders on Yugoslavia, Austria, Switzerland, and France.
> C •  Italy has two large islands:  Sicily and Sardinia.
> T •  The capital of Italy is Rome.
> S •  Some major cities are Rome, Naples, Venice, Florence, and Milan.

## PART 1:
## Geography and Climate of Italy

This southern European country has many different land forms. The mainland of Italy is shaped like a boot.  Italy also includes many islands.  Sicily and Sardinia are two of the largest Italian islands.

Almost four-fifths of Italy is made up of mountains and hills.  In the north, the Alps cut Italy off from the rest of Europe.  They are Italy's tallest mountains. The Apennine Mountains stretch from north to south across most of Italy.

Italy also has many active *volcanoes.* Volcanoes are mountains through which melted rock from deep in the Earth's center has exploded.  The word *volcano* is actually an Italian word.

There are two important areas of Italy that are mostly level plains.  One area surrounds the Po River.  The other area is in the "heel" of the boot in southern Italy.  It is called Apulia. These plains have a great deal of fertile land.

**Map Study:** *Name four countries that border on northern Italy. Italy is shaped like a boot. What is the island at the knee of the boot? at the toe of the boot? Name two important cities in the north of Italy. Name two important cities in the south of Italy.*

## Italy Is a Peninsula

Italy is a *peninsula* surrounded by the Mediterranean Sea. It has 2,685 miles of coastline. Being so close to the ocean has shaped Italy's culture. Many fine harbors dot its coast. For centuries, Italian fishermen have taken advantage of this. Other cultures have also sailed into these harbors and settled here. We can still see the influence of many of these cultures today. The sea has been Italy's route to the rest of the world. The Italians used the sea to bring their culture to many other nations around the world.

## Climate Is Influenced by the Mediterranean

In general, Italy has a *Mediterranean climate.* Its summers are dry and hot. In most areas, Italian winters are usually mild. This kind of climate is caused by the warm temperatures in the Mediterranean Sea.

The weather is also influenced by warm winds that rise from the Sahara Desert in Africa.

Italians like the warm weather. Farmers here have a longer growing season. Vacationers can enjoy Italy's many beaches, as they may have done since the time of the Roman Empire.

*Italians often enjoy swimming and other water sports at their country's many beaches that border on the Mediterranean.*

## Northern Italy Has Colder Winters

The Alps protect Northern Italy from the colder weather in Switzerland and Austria. However, the winters in Northern Italy are still much colder than winters in the south. The north also gets more rain during the winter than other parts of Italy.

This makes the north a perfect area for agriculture. Farmers in the Po River Valley can depend on receiving enough rain to make their crops grow well.

R
E
V
I
E
W

**Directions:**
Number your paper from 1 to 4. Answer the following questions.
1. Which of Italy's geographic areas would be best for farming?
2. Why does most of the world use the Italian term *volcano* to describe an "exploding" mountain?
3. How has Italy's closeness to the sea affected its culture?
4. What two geographic forms outside Italy influence Italy's climate?

# SPOTLIGHT
S T O R Y

## Venice

**V**enice is a very important city in the north of Italy. It is on the coast of the Adriatic Sea. As a matter of fact, it is almost part of the sea.

Venice is actually built on a lagoon. A lagoon is a shallow pond that is near a larger body of water. Venice is built on a collection of marshy islands in the lagoon.

At first, the only people that lived in Venice were fugitives. Most of them were early Christians who were being persecuted on the mainland. They fled to the lagoon, where they would be safe. Eventually, they learned how to live there.

Others soon followed. Using a great deal of cleverness, they built gorgeous churches and fine homes. They had to find a way to build a strong foundation, or basis, for their homes, so they drove huge, uncut trees deep into the silty soil of the marsh. These timbers still hold up many of the original buildings. However, their basements are usually filled with water.

There are a few narrow streets in Venice, and over 400 bridges. The bridges connect the tiny islands. But people have to use boats to get around most of the city. Cars, trucks and buses cannot use the few narrow roads in this city.

One of the most famous boats the Venetians use is called a *gondola*. By law, these boats must be 35 feet long and 4.5 feet wide. They can hold up to five people. The boats are propelled by a gondolier. The gondoliers use a huge oar to paddle their boats through the canals of Venice.

*Gondolas are the taxi-cabs of Venice.*

**Stop and Review**

Write the answers to these questions on your paper.

1. Where in Italy is Venice located?
2. On what type of land is Venice built?
3. Who were the first people to live in Venice? Why did they settle there?
4. How did the people build a strong foundation, or basis, for their homes?
5. How do people in Venice travel through the city?

## PART 2:
## History of Italy

Rome is in the center of the Italian mainland. At one time, it was also the center of the known world.

No one is sure how Rome began. There are many legends about this. But we do know that by about 600 B.C., a group of people called the Latins were living in this city.

Rome grew more powerful as the years went by. The city had many enemies. Most tried to control the city. They did not succeed. By 390 B.C., Rome ruled the entire Italian peninsula. This strong city wanted to expand its land. The Romans fought for new territory to add to their growing *republic*. By the time of the birth of Christ, Rome had built an empire that included a large part of Europe. Within the next 150 years, Rome had conquered lands in Africa and Asia. Parts of these lands all became Roman *provinces*.

### The Roman Empire

The Romans carried their culture with them wherever they went. Their language was called *Latin*. Latin became the language that many people in the conquered lands adopted. Most importantly, the Romans brought a unified government to most of these lands. Their type of government was called a *republic*. The Romans had one leader. At first, this leader was a king. Later, as the empire grew, Rome was ruled by a series of emperors. The emperor had to consult with another group, the *Senate*, before acting. There were 300 senators. Another lawmaking group, called the *Consilium Plebis* represented the people.

---

### Roman Numerals

Today, the numbers that we use are Arabic numbers. In the Roman world, this was not the case.

The Romans used a different number system. Today, we call these numbers Roman numerals. To designate "one," the Romans used I. Two was II. Three was III. Four was IIII, or IV. IV means "one before five." V was the way Romans wrote "five." The Romans used X for "ten."

People throughout the Roman Empire adopted this number system. They used it for many years. Eventually, they found it was too hard to add and subtract using these numbers. So they adopted the Arabic number system we use today.

However, Roman numerals are still in use today. Clocks often use them on their faces. Even the Super Bowls are numbered using Roman numerals!

---

*Ancient Romans built many roads throughout their empire. This one is called the Appian Way. It still exists today.*

## Rome Falls

Rome and its provinces enjoyed a time of great peace, lasting from 27 B.C. to 180 A.D. Then, Rome was the most powerful country in the world. No one challenged its power. This time was called the *Pax Romana*, meaning "Roman peace."

Gradually, Rome began to lose some of its power and unity. Over the next 200 years, it had many internal problems. The once-strong government began to crumble. Its army grew weak. Tribes from northern Europe invaded the empire. By 410, these tribes had entered Rome and destroyed the city. The Roman Empire finally fell in 476, when German Barbarian Odoacer defeated the last emperor of Rome.

## Italy Loses its Unity

Rome was the center that held Italy together. When Rome fell, so did a unified Italy. For the next 1,400 years, the Italian nation did not exist. Countries, people, and even popes fought to control the Italian peninsula.

In the north, cities such as Milan, Pisa, and Venice grew powerful. They thought of themselves as independent countries. The Catholic Church controlled the center of the country. This area was called the *Papal States*. The southern part of Italy was held by foreign countries.

## The Fight for Italian Independence

By the 1850s, many Italians began to believe in a dream. They wanted their country to be free. This idea was known as "Risorgimento." It means "rising again" in Italian.

This new idea got a great deal of support from many different places. Leaders from the independent republic on Sardinia helped unify the Italians. France sent troops to help Sardinia. In 1860, Italian patriots led by Giuseppe Garibaldi landed in Sicily. The three groups fought together to push Austrian and French rulers out of the territory they considered to be their own.

The kingdom of Italy was formed. In 1861, its first king was crowned. His name was Victor Emmanuel II.

**Italy During the World Wars**

Italy fought on the side of the *Allies* during World War I. The Allied nations included France, Great Britain, Russia, and the United States. The Allies won this war, but Italy suffered greatly. Its economy was destroyed. The people in Italy had few jobs and little money. Soon, they began to strike for better living conditions.

In this turmoil, one man emerged as a national leader. His name was Benito Mussolini. He led a group of secret police called the *Blackshirts*. Their terrorism helped Mussolini gain control of Italy in 1922. Mussolini adopted a form of government known as *fascism*. Under fascism, the central government controlled everything — from the newspapers to the factories. Mussolini ruled as a dictator. He was known as *Il Duce*.

It means "The Leader" in Italian. He alone made all government decisions.

Mussolini brought Italy into World War II. Italy fought on the side of Germany as an Axis Power. The Axis Powers were defeated. Not all of Italy had supported Mussolini. After the war, Italians who fought with the Allies captured Il Duce and shot him.

**Italy Today**

On June 2, 1946, Italians voted to establish a republic once again. The new republic grew economically. American aid helped rebuild industry.

Today, Italy has many of the problems that industrial countries share. Inflation has hurt Italy. Unemployment and pollution are also a problem.

Northern Italy has become one of the leading industrial areas in Europe. Industrial development in southern Italy has lagged behind. The government has started many programs to help the south.

REVIEW

**Directions:**
Number your paper from 1 to 5. Answer the following questions.
1. What city was the center of Italian culture before the birth of Christ?
2. What form of government did the Roman Empire have?
3. How did Rome spread its culture through Europe, Asia, and Africa?
4. When did Italy win back its independence after the Roman Empire fell?
5. Describe the type of government Italy had under Mussolini.

## PART 3:
## Language and the Arts

The Romans' language was called *Latin*. It was spoken everywhere. It was a link that united all parts of the empire. The Romans knew that language is a very important part of culture. People who speak the same language are better able to understand each other. They appreciate each others' ideas and feel that they have a common bond.

### Italian Is Based on Latin

Italian is spoken by today's Italians. It is based on Latin. So are many of the other modern European languages, called *Romance languages*. Some other Romance languages are Spanish and French.

The Italian that is spoken today is a form of a dialect that grew up in the Tuscany region of Italy. The Tuscan form of Italian is taught in schools throughout the country. But many Italians still speak different forms of the main language.

### The Renaissance in Italy

During the 1300s, Europe entered a period called the *Renaissance*. It was a time when people were very interested in arts and learning. Great artists did some of their finest work during this time. The Renaissance began in Italy.

During the Renaissance, Italian architects designed many beautiful buildings. They followed the classic and simple lines that Greeks had used years before. Sculptors created beautiful marble statues. Painters, musicians, and writers experimented with new forms.

### Some Italian Words

| English | Italian | Pronunciation |
|---|---|---|
| Please | Per favore | Payr fah-vo´-ray |
| Thank | Grazie | Grat´-see-ay |
| You're welcome | Prego | Pray´-go |
| Good-bye | Arrivederci | Ar-ree-vay-dehr´-chee |

## Michelangelo

Michelangelo was one of the most famous painters and sculptors of the Italian Renaissance. Today people still enjoy looking at his simple and effective works, including his marble statue called *David.* Michelangelo also painted the ceilings of the Sistine Chapel. This chapel is one of the ancient buildings in Vatican City. Recently, these paintings have been restored. People are amazed at their brilliance and artistry.

## Opera

Italy is the birthplace of *opera.* This is a kind of play. Instead of saying lines, the actors in an opera sing them. Many famous Italians have composed great operas that are still performed today.

*The statue of the Pieta is one of Michelangelo's most famous works.*

The first opera ever written was called *Dafne.* It was written in 1597, about the time the first English settlers were coming to the American colonies. The word "opera" is Italian; it means "a work." It is a shorter form of the word "opera in musica," which means a work in music.

Operas are very complicated. They usually have many singers, and their costumes and sets are quite lavish. The stories told by operas are often filled with passionate emotions.

Italy still maintains its commitment to this art form. One of the world's best-known opera companies still performs in Milan. It is called Teatro alla Scala, or simply, La Scala.

*Italians are known all over the world for the colorful and expressive clothes they design and wear.*

## The Arts Today

Italian artists continue to explore new forms of art. Many of them find practical ways to express themselves. Italians design and produce some of the finest race cars in the world. The Ferrari and the Maserati are two of these sleek cars.

Italians have always had a talent for designing clothing. Today, many people throughout the world enjoy the colorful and expressive clothes created by Italian firms such as Benetton.

**R E V I E W**

**Directions:**
Number your paper from 1 to 5. Answer the following questions.
1. What two languages are the basis of modern-day Italian?
2. Name two Romance languages.
3. How would you describe the Renaissance?
4. What is opera?
5. Name two practical ways that Italian artists today express themselves.

# PART 4:
## Life In Modern Italy

The *lira* is the basic unit of the Italian money system. In 1989, Italians had to spend about 1,350 lire to buy an American dollar.

A majority of Italians earn their lire (the plural form of lira) by working in Italy's industries. Most industry is located in the north of Italy. The Italian government owns or controls many industries. For example, it owns most of the large banks and the largest steel factories.

The numbers of Italians working on farms have begun to fall. In 1984, about 15 percent of workers were farmers.

Wheat
Grapes/Wine
Citrus fruit
Rice
Tourism
Industry
Port
Sheep
Diary
Oil
Natural gas
Fishing

**Map Study:** *What symbol does this map use for tourism? What symbol is used for the dairy industry? Would you be more likely to find citrus fruits grown in Milan or Taranto? What kind of economic activity takes place near Leghorn? Name two agricultural products grown on Sicily.*

### Entertainment

Most Italians enjoy many outside activities. They have a good climate for outdoor enjoyment. The Italian coast is lined with great beaches. Swimming, spear-fishing, and scuba diving are some favorite Italian sports.

Soccer, or *calcio*, is almost a national passion. Some people say that if you throw a ball to an American child, he will hit it with a stick. If you throw the ball to an Italian child, he will kick it. There are over 6,000 soccer clubs throughout Italy. There are also many professional soccer

*Italy's mild climate lets Italians enjoy a number of outdoor activities.*

---

## Bocce

Bocce has been an Italian game for many years. Even the Romans played it!

Bocce is played on a special court. It is long and narrow. Usually it is covered with cinders. Two teams play against each other. There can be as many as four players on a team.

Each team has four balls. They are the size of grapefruit. One of the four balls is special. It is called the *pallino*. It is smaller than the other balls.

The game starts when the first player rolls the pallino to the opposite end of the court. The other people on the team then roll their balls. They try to get their balls as close to the pallino as they can. Then the other team takes its turn. The members of this team try to knock their opponents' balls away from the pallino. The team gets points for getting their own balls closest to the pallino.

Bocce used to be a game for old people to play. However, young people in Italy today are becoming interested in it. They watch and play bocce for hours.

---

players. The Italians follow their soccer games with as much interest as Americans watch football and baseball.

Bicycle riding and racing, and auto racing are also popular in Italy.

### Celebrations

Some say that the Roman Empire fell because the people had too many holidays to celebrate. Most Italians would say this was nonsense. After all, what is life without celebrating?

In addition to such traditional holidays as Christmas and Easter, the Italians celebrate several other days. Many towns in Italy have a patron saint, or holy person, with whom the people feel a special bond. Each year, the town will have a festival to honor their saint.

However, the origin of other feast days is not as well known. For example, the people who live in the town of Marostica in northern Italy hold a special chess game. It is played in front of a medieval castle. The chess pieces are actually people from the town, dressed up in fantastic costumes. As the game is played they move about the huge board in the town square in a life-sized game of chess.

Another regional festival is called the Palio. It is held in the town of Siena, which is also part of northern Italy. The people first hold a parade through the town. All the people wear costumes that make them look like they are living in the Middle Ages. Some even wear suits of armor. After a parade, there is a horse race, held in the tiny village square. The horses gallop through the square, making sharp turns at great speed. Sometimes, this causes the riders to fall off. It does not matter, though. The winner is the first horse to cross the finish line — with or without a rider! Thousands of people come to see this event, which is held twice a year.

Which event would you be most interested in seeing?

**Religion**

Italy has always been tied to the Roman Catholic Church. The head of the Catholic Church is the Pope. The Pope lives in an independent country that is inside Rome. It is called Vatican City.

Today, over 95 percent of the Italian people belong to the Catholic Church.

*In many Italian towns, the local Catholic Church is the largest and most impressive building.*

*In certain parts of Italy, particularly the south, people's beliefs and way of life have changed very little over the years.*

if they have a problem, the Italians will go to their family priest to find help.

Some religious traditions in the country combine pagan ways with the ways of the Church. For example, in the south of Italy, women in remote villages sometimes go into fits of hysteria. The people in the villages think that they have been bitten by poisonous spiders of the devil called tarantole. They will bring these women to the village priest so that he can "cure" them. Another "cure" the villagers might suggest would be for a victim to dance the tarantella — a lively folk dance that is supposed to take away the evil from the bite of the spider.

Which cure would you suggest?

The Catholic Church is the center of religious life for most Italians. It is also the center of much of their social and cultural life as well, particularly in the rural areas of the country. People love to attend parties and festivals sponsored by the Church throughout the year. And,

## Other Superstitions

The bite of the tarantole is just one of the superstitions held by people in rural areas of Italy, particularly in the south. Many people there believe in the power of the "evil eye." Those who have "the evil eye" are supposed to be able to harm other people just by looking at them. According to tradition, the person who has this power can use it to cause illness and even death. People also believe you must do special things to protect yourself from those who have the evil eye. Some say prayers when they are near these people; others wear jewelry of a certain color.

If you want good luck, the Italians think you should eat gnocchi on September 29. (Gnocchi are small, round potato dumplings.)

And, if you want to impress your Italian girlfriends, never bring them chrysanthemums. The Italians use them only for funerals.

## Family Life in Italy

Many of you probably feel very close to your family. This is the way most Italians feel. There is nothing in their life that is more important to them than their families. Rich or poor, it makes no difference. Whatever they have, they will gladly give to other members of their family. And, if that means sharing an apartment with grandparents, aunts, uncles, and cousins, so be it. Most Italian homes have a special room called the tinello, where the family

*Italy is a place where old and new often meet.*

*Because of Italy's hilly terrain, there are very few level places where people can build homes. This means that many houses are often crowded together in a small area.*

eats and meets after school and work is over. The more formal salotta is reserved for entertaining guests.

This spirit of warmth also extends to their friends. When friends meet in the street, they will usually kiss each other on the cheek and hug. Men will walk hand-in-hand while they stroll through the town piazza, catching up on the latest news and people-watching. You probably would not be comfortable with this kind of contact, but it is very important to an Italian.

## Education

All Italian children must attend school from ages six through fourteen. Most schools are run by the government. There are also private schools.

In high school, Italian students have two choices. Many attend a *liceo*. This is a high school where they study language and arts. Others choose to attend a technical institute, where they train for a specific career.

What would it be like to go to school in Italy? Attending school in Italy is much like going to school in the United States. But there are some important differences between the two.

For example, Italian students usually wear uniforms. Every elementary school has a different uniform, so each student in a school wears the same thing. Boys may have to wear a white shirt. Girls might wear a white blouse or a blue smock. Both boys and girls may wear a red tie as part of their school uniform.

All students go home for lunch, because their school day ends around 1:00 P.M. However, they make up this time by going to school on Saturdays.

Most schools do not have playgrounds. Students do not usually play school sports, either.

Do you think you would like to attend school in Italy?

## Italian Cooking

Well-cooked, good food is a strong part of the Italian culture. Italians delight in preparing special foods for their family and guests. They are always urging them to "mangia!" This means "eat!" in Italian.

Italian cooks prepare a wide variety of dishes. Each region of Italy has a special way to prepare the food for which they are famous. For example, Milan is known for its minestrone soup.

Did you know that Italians eat a great deal of veal and pasta? Veal is meat that comes from young beef cattle. Pasta is made from wheat, eggs, and water.

If you were to eat a meal in Italy, some of the specialties you might sample would include gnocchi (potato-filled dumplings), polenta (a mushy corn meal), osso busco (a veal stew made with tomatoes), or cannelloni (pasta tubes filled with meat).

## Polenta

Polenta is a dish that is prepared in Northern Italy. It can be served in two ways: either fried and served with a cream or tomato sauce, or as a side dish with an entree. Polenta that has not been fried has a mushy consistency, like grits. Whichever way you decide to serve it, polenta ideally should be made with coarsely-ground corn meal. However, regular corn meal will work also.

Ingredients:
1 T. salt
2 cups (1/2 liter) coarsely-ground corn meal
8 T. olive oil

Directions:
Add 1 T. of salt to 7 cups (1-1/2 liters) of boiling water. Slowly stir in cornmeal in a thin, steady stream. Cook for 20 minutes. Stir occasionally. When the polenta is stiff and pulls away from the side of the pot, it is done. Spread polenta in a baking dish. It can be kept warm in a 250° (120° C) oven and served as a side dish. If you prefer your polenta fried, let it cool in the refrigerator. Once it is cool, cut into squares and fry lightly in olive oil.

**R E V I E W**

**Directions:**
Number your paper from 1 to 5. Answer the following questions.
1. How do most Italians earn their money?
2. What are some water sports that Italians enjoy?
3. How popular is soccer in Italy?
4. To what religion do most Italians belong?
5. Name one Italian dish that you would enjoy eating.

# MAP SKILLS

# LATITUDE

Mapmakers have created a series of imaginary lines that mark the Earth. The lines that go around the Earth are called lines of latitude. They are parallel to the equator. They help the map reader find places on the map. Latitude is measured in degrees. The symbol for degrees is °.

**Directions:** Choose the correct latitude for these Italian cities. Use the map to help you find the answers.

1. Palermo's latitude is (40°, 38°) north.
2. Rome's latitude is near (42°, 16°) north.
3. Como's latitude is near (10°, 46°) north.
4. Bologna is near (44°, 109°) north latitude.
5. Venice is near (38°, 46°) north latitude.
6. Naples and (Milan, Bari) are located at about the same latitude.
7. Genoa and (Bologna, Como) are located at about the same latitude.
8. Como and (Venice, Genoa) are located at about the same latitude.

# CHAPTER 3 REVIEW

## Summary of Italy

*Italian culture has been shaped by many factors, including geography and climate. For example, the Italians have learned to live on a land that is very hilly.*

*One important influence on Italian culture was the Roman Empire. The Romans also brought their culture to other areas of the world. When German tribes conquered the Romans, the empire fell apart. For the next 1400 years, Italy was a divided and weak country.*

*Italy declared its independence in 1861. In this century, the Italians fought in both World Wars. Benito Mussolini's fascist government emerged from the economic chaos following World War I.*

*Italians today speak a language that is based on the Latin the Romans spoke. They share this cultural heritage with other languages, such as French, that are based on Latin.*

*Italian culture is rich with the contributions from many artists. The great reawakening of interest in the arts that we call the Renaissance began in Italy during the Middle Ages. Today, Italian artists continue to express themselves by designing classic racing cars and fine clothing.*

*Most Italians earn their lire by working in the nation's industries. They share a great love for well-prepared food. In their free time, Italians enjoy soccer and many other outdoor sports.*

## Critical Thinking Skills

**Directions:** Give some serious thought to the questions below. Be sure to answer in complete sentences.

1. Italy is surrounded on three sides by water. How has this influenced the Italian culture?
2. Do you think the Roman culture helped or hurt European culture in general? Give two reasons for your decision.

3. How did the Italians achieve independence in 1861?
4. In your opinion, why do most Italians enjoy playing or watching soccer?
5. What part has the Roman Catholic Church played in Italian culture over the years?

## For Discussion

**Directions:** Discuss these questions with your class. Appoint one class member to write the ideas you discover on the board.

1. What are some of the advantages and disadvantages of having the government own and control a large part of Italy's industries?
2. What factors in Italy's politics and economy made it possible for a ruler like Benito Mussolini to emerge as a national leader? Do you see any modern countries where the same problems are happening?
3. If you were an Italian high school student, would you choose to attend a liceo or a technical institute? Compare the advantages of each system.

## Write It!

**Directions:** You are planning a dinner for your Italian friend. You want her to feel at home. You will be serving Italian dishes. Plan and write a menu for the dinner. Use a cookbook to help you.

## For You To Do

**Directions:** Italians are known for their love of clean and expressive designs in clothes and automobiles. Design a special outfit or a racing car that you feel best meets the Italian goals of design. Display your designs on a class bulletin board.

# THE UNITED KINGDOM

## Chapter 4

F
A
C
T
S

- The United Kingdom is near the western edge of Europe.
- It includes England, Scotland, Wales, and Northern Ireland.
- The United Kingdom is surrounded by water.
- It is one of the most densely populated countries in the world.
- The official language of the United Kingdom is English.

## PART 1:
## Geography and Climate of the United Kingdom

The United Kingdom is made up of the countries of England, Scotland, Wales, and Northern Ireland.

The United Kingdom is set apart from the rest of Europe by water. The English Channel is only 34 miles wide. It separates the United Kingdom from France. Today, people easily cross from one country to the next. They use hydroplanes to make a fast trip.

However, this was not always the case. At times, the water that surrounds the United Kingdom has protected the island nation. Today's British culture has been shaped by this separation. For the past 1,000 years, no one has invaded this land.

The sea has always been Britain's route to the world. No point on the United Kingdom is more than 75 miles from the sea. At one time, the British navy was the best in the world.

# THE UNITED KINGDOM

**Map Study:** *The United Kingdom is made up of four countries: England, Scotland, Wales, and Northern Ireland. Which country in the United Kingdom is the farthest north? Which country in the United Kingdom is closest to France? In which country of the United Kingdom is the city of Leeds? Edinburgh? Newport? Belfast? Coventry?*

## The Geography of the United Kingdom Is Varied

The United Kingdom includes many different kinds of land forms.

In the north and the west, there are *highlands*. They are regions of mountains, deep valleys, and *plateaus*. Most of the highlands are *moors*. Moors are desolate places. Only a few plants grow on the moors. The soil is very poor. Few people live in the highlands.

The Pennine Mountains are a major geographic feature of Great Britain. They stretch from Scotland through central England. Great Britain is another name for the United Kingdom.

The English lowlands are south of the Pennines. This is the area where most of Great Britain's agriculture and industry have developed.

The United Kingdom also has many wide rivers and lakes. In Scotland, the lakes are called *lochs*. In Northern Ireland, they are called *loughs*.

Its ships brought British citizens to all parts of the globe. The British once controlled an *empire* that covered about one-fourth of the world's land. They traveled easily from place to place. They brought the British culture to many different areas of the world.

## The United Kingdom Has a Mild Climate

The United Kingdom is farther north than Labrador. But its climate is not as extreme as you would expect. Its weather is influenced by the ocean. There is a current of warm water that flows past Ireland and Great Britain. It is called the *North Atlantic Current.* In

*Moors are desolate places in the highlands where few people live and very little grows.*

the winter, the current warms the west winds that blow over the United Kingdom. In summer, the current cools these winds. This means that the climate in the United Kingdom is never too hot or too cold.

## Rainfall

These warm winds also bring a great deal of rain to the United Kingdom. Most rain falls in the western parts of the country. Some of these areas get as much as 200 inches of rain a year.

Rain is a constant part of the weather forecast in the United Kingdom. Forecasters on the television often report the number of hours they expect the sun will shine during the day.

There is a "silver lining" for all these rain clouds: the constant rain is helpful to British farmers. Crops grow very well in this kind of climate.

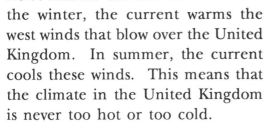

**Directions:**
Number your paper from 1 to 5. Answer the following questions.
1. How has the English Channel shaped British culture?
2. How did the British use the sea to build their empire?
3. What are moors?
4. Why do few people live on the moors?
5. How does the British climate help farmers here?

## PART 2:
## History of the United Kingdom

Scholars know that people have been living in England for over 10,000 years. They probably came from other parts of Europe. We know some of the details about the culture that developed here. For example, they built large stone monuments. Stonehenge is one of these monuments. This circle of giant stones is still standing today. No one is exactly sure how the culture used these monuments.

---

### The Scottish Tartan

Many people have seen Scottish groups in parades and other exhibitions. The people in the group usually wear a kilt of plaid fabric. Sometimes, they wear a matching scarf. These garments are part of the traditions of Scotland.

They are made out of a fabric called tartan. At one time, many people throughout the United Kingdom, including the Scots, wore tartans. Each tribe, or clan, had its own tartan. It had a special pattern of stripes, called a sett. Only people in the clan could wear that tartan.

Today, many people enjoy wearing clothes made with a certain tartan. Even the royal family of the United Kingdom has a special tartan for its use. It is called Royal Stewart.

---

About 500 years before the birth of Christ, *Celts* from the mainland of Europe invaded England. These invaders conquered the tribes that lived in England. Gradually, these tribes adopted the culture and traditions of the Celts.

### Rome Makes England a Colony

About 50 years before the birth of Christ, Roman soldiers first came to England. The island was then known as Brittania. The great Roman general Julius Caesar brought his troops to the island. At first, the Romans just wanted to explore the territory.

Caesar reported what he had found to the Roman emperor Claudius. Claudius decided that the island would make a good addition to his empire. He sent more soldiers to Britannia. They easily defeated the Celts. England became part of the Roman Empire.

Rome controlled England for over 400 years. During this time, England grew stronger and stronger. Roman soldiers protected the Celts from their neighbors to the north, the Scots. They built walls and roads to

# SPOTLIGHT
## S T O R Y

## Stonehenge

Stonehenge is an ancient monument located in the southern part of Great Britain. It is a group of large, roughly-cut stones. These boulders are approximately 13 feet tall and weigh about 28 tons each. Time has taken its toll on this monument. Many of the original stones have been removed. People are no longer allowed to walk in the monument. The British government is concerned that they will damage the stones even more.

No one can be sure how and why the monument was built. Scientists say it was constructed over 3,500 years ago. But nobody knows how people at the time used this area.

One man has a theory about the reason Stonehenge was built. His name is Gerald S. Hawkins. Hawkins' theory is that the monument was built as a giant calendar. Some stones in this group mark the places where the moon and sun rose and set on certain days of the year. These days were December 21 and June 21. Today we know that these days mark the start of winter and summer. December 21 is called the winter solstice. In the northern hemisphere, there are fewer hours of sunlight on this day than on any other. June 21 is called the summer solstice. In the northern hemisphere, there are more hours of sunlight on this day than on any other.

However, we may never actually know if Hawkins is right.

### Stop and Review
Write the answers to these questions on your paper.
1. What is Stonehenge?
2. Why are people no longer allowed to walk through Stonehenge?
3. How long ago was Stonehenge built?
4. What is Hawkin's theory about Stonehenge?
5. When is the winter solstice?

*Parts of Stonehenge were built of stones that are only found in western Wales. How do you think those stones were brought here?*

connect their military camps. English people took advantage of the road system to trade more and more goods with people who lived in other parts of their country. Roman culture became English culture. Their Latin language was adopted by many Celts. It became the language of scholars.

## Life in a Medieval Castle

What would it have been like to live in a medieval castle? Chances are you would have spent most of your time in the keep, or the donjon. This is where the lord of the castle and his family lived. It featured a great hall that served as everything from dining room to bedroom. The lord, his family, and all their servants, ate, entertained, and slept there. Each castle had its own chapel, and usually its own priest to conduct services there. The castle held storehouses for food and weapons, stables for horses and other animals, and even a prison for captured enemies. These buildings were enclosed by strong, thick stone walls. Sometimes, a moat encircled the outside of the castle walls. The moat could be filled with water, or be left dry. There were very few windows in a castle. Windows let in the rain and snow and were weak places in a castle's defense. Instead, castles had long, narrow slits in the wall for windows, where archers could shoot their arrows at the enemy below.

Do you think you would have liked to live in a medieval castle?

## Tribes From Germany Invade the Island

England's early history continued to be shaped by invaders. Around the year 400, tribes from Germany started to invade the Roman Empire. The Romans called the troops back to defend their city. England lost the protection the soldiers had given them. Picts from Scotland swarmed into England. Other tribes from Germany also took advantage of the situation. They invaded England and quickly conquered the people there. The *Jutes*, *Angles*, and *Saxons* built permanent settlements throughout the country. England became known as *Angle-land*. The Angles and Saxons soon became the most powerful tribes in Angle-land. They developed a system of seven separate, loosely united kingdoms. The system was known as the *Heptarchy*.

During the 800s, Danes invaded England. They conquered six of the kingdoms. Only the kingdom of Wessex, led by King Alfred the Great, resisted their attacks. He pushed the Danes into northern England. This area became known as *Danelaw*.

Alfred became one of the greatest leaders England had ever known. He unified the other kingdoms, built the first great English *fleet*, and organized local governments throughout England. *Common law* first developed under Alfred's rule. This principle became the basis of laws in many other countries, including the United States.

After Alfred died, the Danes gradually extended their kingdom. They soon controlled the entire area.

*When the Normans conquered England in 1066, they brought many changes to English culture, such as the custom of building heavily fortified castles. In a time when neighbors fought against each other for control of the land, castles were very necessary.*

### French Forces Invade England

The last Saxon king died without an heir. The noble people in the country chose Harold, the Earl of Essex, to be king. But a French nobleman named William said that the king had promised him that he would be king. William decided to press his claim to the throne. He led a large army of soldiers from Normandy in an invasion of England. Normandy is a region in northwestern France. In 1066, this army killed King Harold and defeated the Saxons at the Battle of Hastings. On Christmas Day, William the Conqueror was crowned King of England.

William brought French culture to England. He built many castles and cathedrals. He organized a strong central government. At first, the Anglo-Saxons resisted the French culture. They kept their own language and customs. Gradually, there was a change. The two groups adopted cultural traits from each other. The differences between the two were gradually erased.

### The Struggle for Power

The invasion led by William was the last one that would shape English culture. From this point on, the English controlled their own culture and history.

This time was marked by many struggles for control of the government. Throughout this era, many kings emerged to lead the country.

They had almost absolute power. Other noblemen fought for some say in government affairs. In 1215, they forced King John to sign the *Magna Carta*. This document gave the nobles many rights. The rights contained in the Magna Carta have been the basis for the rights of citizens in many other governments, including our own.

England continued to grow as a world power. Under Elizabeth I, the English established colonies in the New World. The English navy grew even stronger. When it defeated the Spanish fleet in 1588, England became the ruler of the seas.

## Great Britain Is Established

The United Kingdom was actually formed in 1707. Unlike so many other events in English history, it was accomplished peacefully. The *Parliament* of England and Wales, and the Parliament of Scotland signed an Act of Union. This law joined the three nations under one government.

The young government had one large problem. It resulted from their earlier exploration in the New World. Their colonies in America wanted to be free from Great Britain. The war, and the eventual independence of the colonies, cost Great Britain

dearly. However, Britain soon established friendly relations with the newly formed United States. Trade between the two flourished.

## The Industrial Revolution

Great Britain continued to grow in importance. This time their growth came from within. British people began to discover new, faster ways to manufacture goods using machines driven by water or steam. This was the start of a movement that changed economies throughout the world. It became known as the *Industrial Revolution*. Great Britain profited greatly from these advances. Her position as a world leader was guaranteed by her powerful economy. This power allowed Great Britain's empire of colonies throughout the world to grow and flourish.

## Great Britain During the World Wars

During both world wars, Britain headed a group of nations called the *Allies*. These countries included France, the United States, and many others. The Allies fought against Germany and the nations that had joined Germany to fight for control of Europe. In both World War I and World War II, the Allies were the victors. But the cost to Great Britain was very high. Many British soldiers died in both wars. During World War II, the Germans bombed London and many other cities in Great Britain. The British economy was destroyed. These wars cost Great Britain its place as a leading nation in the world.

## Modern Great Britain

However, Great Britain struggled to rebuild itself and its economy. Today, this nation has emerged as one of the most developed countries in Europe. It has become a leading nation in Europe. In 1973, it joined a loose union of European countries called the *European Economic Community.* Members of this group, called

*The British rebuilt Coventry Cathedral after World War II. However, they left the damaged church still standing to show how far this culture had come in recovering from the effects of World War II.*

the EEC, give each other certain trading advantages.

Today, Britain is led by Prime Minister Margaret Thatcher. She is the first woman to ever hold this position.

**Directions:**
Number your paper from 1 to 6. Answer the following questions.
1. How did Roman control help England?
2. Why were Picts from Scotland and tribes from Germany able to invade England?
3. How did Alfred the Great unify England?
4. When and how was Great Britain formed?
5. What was the Industrial Revolution? How did it change Great Britain's economy?
6. What is the EEC?

## PART 3:
## Language, the Arts, and Inventions

Today, most people in Great Britain speak English. This language developed over many centuries. Its roots were in the languages spoken by the people who invaded this country, including the Normans from France, and the German tribes called the Angles and the Saxons. Language experts classify English as part of the Germanic family of languages.

Some people in Great Britain do speak other languages. About one-fourth of the people in Wales speak Welsh. Originally, Welsh was a Celtic language. Many Scots speak another form of Celtic called Gaelic. Some Irish people also speak a different form of Gaelic.

In the 1500s, fewer than 2 million people spoke English. Today, over 450 million people throughout the world use this language. English has the largest vocabulary of any language in the world today. It also has one of the most complicated grammars.

**There Are Many Different Ways of Speaking English**

As in most countries, the way English is spoken differs from region to region. British people who have been educated at the larger universities in the country have a different accent than people living in the western part of the country. The people who live in the East End of London even have a special way of speaking their language. It is called *cockney*.

| Some English Words | |
| --- | --- |
| **"English" English** | **"American" English** |
| lift | elevator |
| chemist | drugstore |
| tube | subway |
| flat | apartment |
| petrol | gasoline |

The English spoken in the United States is very different from the English spoken in Great Britain. We use different words than the British do to describe the same thing.

**Britain Has Produced Some of the World's Greatest Authors**

Great Britain, and England before it, have always played a great part in the development of all of the arts. But their contributions to literature have been, by far, the greatest.

William Shakespeare was born in England. Today many consider him to be the greatest playwright the world has ever known. Other literary leaders from the United Kingdom include Geoffrey Chaucer, John Keats, George Gordon, Lord Byron, Robert Burns, Percy Bysshe Shelley, and Charles Dickens, among many others. Their works are still studied and appreciated by people throughout the world today.

Because the English language is spoken by so many people, many cultures have been able to share the richness of the poems, plays, novels, and stories created by these writers.

**The Arts in Great Britain Today**

Today, literature and many other arts continue to thrive in Britain.

*Simon Rattle conducts the City of Birmingham Symphony Orchestra.*

There are over ten major symphony orchestras in the country, and many smaller ones. London continues to be the center of theater for the entire world. The government takes an active role in the arts. It gives financial help to opera and ballet companies, orchestras, and theaters.

**Inventions**

One of the greatest influences on all world cultures today started in

Great Britain. It was called the Industrial Revolution. This peaceful revolution began with the invention of machines to take the place of people and animals in growing and making goods. Inventors harnessed the power of steam and water. They used these power sources to build huge factories for manufacturing goods. People's lives were changed drastically. Society had been based on farming. Now, people moved off their farms and into the factories. Their entire way of life was changed.

**R E V I E W**

**Directions:**
Number your paper from 1 to 4. Answer the following questions.
1. What languages were the root languages for English?
2. How many people spoke English in 1500? How many speak English today?
3. How does the English government support the arts today?
4. How did the Industrial Revolution change people's lives?

## PART 4:
## Life in the United Kingdom Today

The *pound* is the basic money unit in the United Kingdom. In 1989, a pound was worth about $1.60 in American dollars. The sign the British use for a pound is £.

Most British workers are employed by the nation's manufacturing industry. Great Britain is one of the largest manufacturing nations in the world. Money from manufacturing goods and trading them with other nations could actually support the entire British economy. No one would have to do anything else. Only two percent of the English people work in agriculture and fishing. They produce about half the food needed by the British people. The United Kingdom imports the rest of its food.

**Government Support**

The United Kingdom has a unique form of social support for its people. Each family receives a weekly payment from the government for each of their children that is in school. Doctors' visits and most medical treatments are free or given at reduced rates. Retired workers receive a government pension. All in all, the United Kingdom supports its citizens from birth to death. These services cost the government billions of dollars each year. While some of the money comes from contributions paid by workers, employers, the self-employed, and the wealthy, more than three-quarters of it is collected from taxes.

## Family Life in the United Kingdom

If you visited a family in the United Kingdom, what could you expect to find? First, you would probably enter a small, two-story home, attached to others much like townhouses in the United States. Through the window you could see the neat gardens and lush green lawn in the yard.

The family you might visit would probably be small. Like the United States, the United Kingdom has had a growing divorce rate. People are

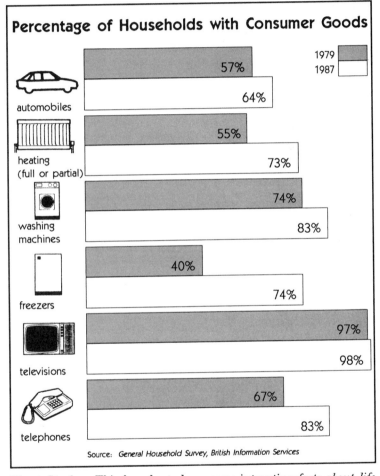

**Percentage of Households with Consumer Goods**

1979
1987

automobiles: 57% (1979), 64% (1987)

heating (full or partial): 55% (1979), 73% (1987)

washing machines: 74% (1979), 83% (1987)

freezers: 40% (1979), 74% (1987)

televisions: 97% (1979), 98% (1987)

telephones: 67% (1979), 83% (1987)

Source: *General Household Survey, British Information Services*

**Chart Study:** *This bar chart shows some interesting facts about life in the United Kingdom today. The bars show what percentage, or parts of 100, of homes there have certain consumer goods. One bar shows the percentage in 1979. The other bar shows the percentage in 1987. For example, in 1979, 97 percent of the homes (97 out of 100 homes) in the United Kingdom had a television set. What percentage of homes had a television set in 1987? In 1979, what percentage of homes had a freezer? Did that percentage go up or down by 1987?*

*New housing in London's Docklands*

also waiting longer to get married, if they do at all. So, your hosts tonight might include a man, a woman, and their small son.

If it were winter, the first thing you would notice would be the temperature. Not all homes in the United Kingdom have central heat; about one-fourth do not. Even if there is central heat, the temperature would probably be closer to 60 degrees Fahrenheit than the more comfortable 72 degrees we usually experience in our homes. Perhaps your host would offer you a warm woolen sweater to wear.

Next, you might be greeted by the family pet, usually a friendly dog. The British are very fond of their pets. Your hosts might offer you a "spot of tea" or some other refreshments. Later on, as you get to know one another, you might chat about

the results of the latest soccer match, or the newest strain of a special flower the family was trying to grow.

The family might also ask you to join them in their favorite evening pastime — watching television. You could watch either the BBC or the IBA networks. The BBC is the British Broadcasting Corporation; the IBA is the Independent Broadcasting Authority. As you watch, you would notice that there are no commercials. Your hosts have paid an annual fee to watch BBC programs. This network does not show any commercials. The IBA shows commercials every half hour. If you could not find anything to watch, the family might also play one of their videotapes for you.

At the end of your visit, you would thank your hosts and leave, having enjoyed a typical evening with a British family.

### Entertainment

The British love sports of all kinds. Soccer, which is called football in the United Kingdom, is popular. Another sport, *cricket*, is sometimes called the national sport. Like baseball, it is played with two teams, a bat, and a ball. However, it has very different rules. Many British people also like to play rugby.

Many people in the United Kingdom take great pride in a sporting event called the Scottish Highland Games. These games test the skills of modern-day athletes at such ancient sports as tossing the caber. A caber is the trunk of a young tree. Young or not, the tree is very heavy! While the athletes compete, so do dancers and musicians. People come from all over the world to these annual games, held in Scottish cities.

The British also love to gamble on sporting events, particularly horse racing. Ninety-four percent of the British people say they have gambled at one time or another.

Many people in the United Kingdom also enjoy gardening. Even the smallest yards are filled with beautiful plants and shrubs. All are carefully tended. Some people even rent land, called an allotment, to raise vegetables.

*Pubs*, or public houses, are also part of the Britain's leisure time. People go to neighborhood pubs to enjoy a glass of ale or a game of darts — or just to catch up on the neighborhood gossip.

## Celebrations

People in Britain celebrate many of the same holidays as your family. Christmas, New Year's Day, and Easter are all important occasions on the British calendar.

The British also celebrate some events that are uniquely their own. Many are based on events in the Royal Family. For example, every June, there is the impressive Trooping of the Colors. In this ceremony, the queen rides past her troops as they stand at attention in their finest dress uniforms.

Another unique British holiday is Guy Fawkes Day, celebrated on November 5. This holiday goes back

### Driving in the U.K.

Driving a car in the United Kingdom can be strange for Americans who visit there. In the first place, the names for parts of the car are different. The hood of the car is called the bonnet; the trunk is called the boot. The windshield is called the wind screen. And petrol, not gas, makes the car run.

By law, the English drive on the left-hand side of the road. In most other countries, people drive on the right. Slow drivers in the United Kingdom are expected to stay in the extreme left-hand lane.

If you do visit the United Kingdom, be on the lookout for "Halt" instead of "Stop" signs, "Diversion" instead of "Detour" signs, and "Zebra crossings." No, there are no animals on the loose. These are the pedestrian crosswalks.

many years. It actually started when Guy Fawkes tried to blow up the Houses of Parliament in 1605. On this holiday, British children make stuffed dummies called guys. They carry them as they go door-to-door, asking for "a penny for the guy." At the end of the day, the children take the dolls and burn them in a huge bonfire. There are also many fireworks displays that evening.

## Religion

The United Kingdom has two official churches. One is the Church of England. It is Episcopalian. The other is the Church of Scotland, which is Presbyterian. Both are part of the Protestant faith. The king or queen of Great Britain must belong to the Church of England.

*Primary school pupils in the United Kingdom enjoy working with computers.*

The Protestant faith in England began under the rule of King Henry VIII. At the time, most English people were Roman Catholic. However, Henry had the Parliament pass a law that said the king, not the pope, was the head of the Church in England. In other countries, religious leaders were also questioning the power of the Roman Catholic Church. This led to the development of many Protestant religions throughout the area. Protestants originally "protested" the Catholic Church.

Today, English people have the freedom to worship as they please, but most of them belong to the Church of England.

## Education

The United Kingdom has three separate education systems. Each takes care of establishing policies in its own geographical area. There is a system for England and Wales, one for Scotland, and one for Northern Ireland.

All children in the United Kingdom must attend school from the ages of five to sixteen. Usually, children attend elementary school until they are eleven. Then, they go on to high school.

Sometimes, the British use terms to describe their schools that do not mean the same thing in the United States. For example, a British grammar school is actually a high school that prepares students to attend college. Public schools in Great Britain are private high schools. Some public schools, such as Eton and Harrow, are centuries old.

The United Kingdom has a number of universities and colleges. Two of the world's most famous universities, Cambridge and Oxford, are located outside of London.

## Eating in the United Kingdom

Traditionally, the British like plain, simple foods. They like meats that are boiled or grilled, and use fewer spices than cooks in other European countries. Today, British people spend less of their income on food than many other Europeans. They tend to purchase foods that are easy to prepare. Microwave ovens have become popular because of the time they can save. British people also use a great deal of take-away food. In the United States, we call this carry-out food. One favorite take-away food is fish and chips. Chips are like French fries.

Sometimes, the British like to pause for tea in the afternoon. This can be a cup of tea and a biscuit, or cookie, or it can also be a full meal, with sandwiches, desserts, and even a main dish. This is called high tea.

If you were to eat a meal in the United Kingdom, some specialties you might taste would be bangers and mash (sausage and mashed potatoes), toad-in-the-hole (sausages baked into pastry), crumpets (a type of "English" muffin), or Cornish pasties (a turnover made with meat and potatoes). For the truly adventurous, there is haggis: a Scottish mixture of a sheep's heart, liver, and lungs, mixed with oatmeal, suet, onions, and spices that is boiled in a sheep's stomach. Which of these British specialties would you like to try?

R E V I E W

**Directions:**
Number your paper from 1 to 5. Answer the following questions.
1. What is the basic money unit in the United Kingdom? In American dollars, how much is a pound worth?
2. How does the welfare system in the United Kingdom support British citizens from birth to death?
3. Name two sports that British people like to play.
4. What are public schools in the United Kingdom?
5. What are take-away foods? Give an example of a traditional British take-away food.

# THE UNITED KINGDOM

## MAP SKILLS

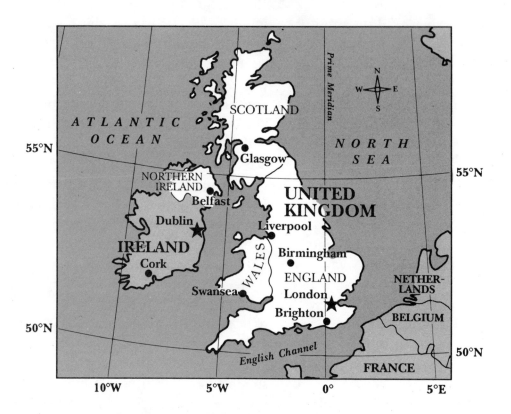

## LONGITUDE

Mapmakers have created a series of imaginary lines that mark the Earth. The lines that go from the North Pole to the South Pole are called lines of longitude. They help the map reader find places on the map. Longitude is measured in degrees. The symbol for degrees is °.

**Directions:** Choose the correct longitude for these places in the United Kingdom. Use the map to help you find the answers.

1. London, England is located near (0°, 150° west) longitude, which is also called the Prime Meridian.

2. Glasgow, Scotland is near (4°, 60°) west longitude.

3. Swansea, Wales is near (40°, 4°) west longitude.

4. Belfast, Northern Ireland is near (80°, 6°) west longitude.

5. Brighton, England is near (0°, 9° west) longitude.

6. Glasgow is on about the same longitude as (Swansea, Brighton).

7. London is located on about the same longitude as (Belfast, Brighton).

8. Birmingham, England is near (2°, 53°) west longitude.

# CHAPTER 4 REVIEW

## Summary of the United Kingdom

*Culture in the United Kingdom has been shaped by many factors. Its four countries share a varied geography and a mild, wet climate. Today's British have a rich culture that has its roots in the cultures that have invaded this land, including the Celts, the Romans, Germanic tribes, and the French.*

*Britain, in turn, has shared her culture with many other countries, including the United States, and other lands that were once part of her great empire. Principles of law and government that developed here are still in use throughout the world. The Industrial Revolution that began in Great Britain completely changed cultures around the world. The world still holds dear the great writings of many British authors.*

*Today, the United Kingdom has emerged from the destruction of two world wars to become a modern industrial and world power. The people in the United Kingdom enjoy an extensive system of social support from the government. Everyday life in the United Kingdom includes many typically British sports, such as rugby and cricket, unique customs, and excellent school systems.*

## Critical Thinking Skills

**Directions:** Give some serious thought to the questions below. Be sure to answer in complete sentences.

1. Why do you think that people who live in the United Kingdom like to vacation in warm, sunny climates?
2. Not very many people live in the highlands in the United Kingdom. Why do you think this is true?
3. How did the Roman occupation change British culture?
4. Great Britain has been known by many different names. List two of these

names. How did they reflect British culture at the time?
5. Why do many people in the United Kingdom usually look for fast and easy ways to prepare their food?

## For Discussion

**Directions:** Discuss these questions with your class. Appoint one class member to write the ideas you discover on the board.

1. What modern techniques make it possible for two percent of the British people to produce half the food their nation consumes?
2. How does the system of providing social support that is used in the United Kingdom compare with the system used today in the United States? Which system seems better to you?

## Write It!

**Directions:** No one knows for sure why Stonehenge was built. There is a theory that it was constructed to serve as a giant calendar. Develop your own theory about the way this ancient monument was used. Write a paragraph that gives your theory and the reasons behind it.

## For You to Do

**Directions:** Shakespeare is one of the United Kingdom's — and the world's — greatest writers. One of his most famous plays is called *Romeo and Juliet*. Find a copy of it in your school library. Read through Act II, Scene II. It is called the "Balcony Scene" because Juliet appears on a balcony outside her room. Choose members of your class to take the part of Romeo and Juliet. Have them act out Act II, Scene II.

# FRANCE

- France is the largest country in Western Europe.
- The capital of France is Paris.
- About 80 percent of France's population lives in urban areas.
- Some major cities are Paris, Lyon, Marseille, Toulouse, and Nice.
- The national anthem of France is called "La Marseillaise."

## PART 1:
## Geography and Climate

A hexagon is a six-sided figure. Many people in France call their country "L'hexagon," because of its shape. On three sides of the hexagon, France has borders with other countries. On the other three sides, France is surrounded by water. All in all, France has a coastline that is about 2,300 miles long.

The ocean to the north and west form parts of France's borders. The Pyrenees Mountains are another natural border. They separate France from Spain. The Alps and Jura Mountains also separate France from Italy and Switzerland.

However, the border that France shares with Belgium, Luxembourg, and West Germany has no natural markers. This has greatly shaped French culture, particularly in modern times. German armies have not had to cross great mountains or ford wide rivers to invade France. French armies have had easy access to other countries in Europe.

# FRANCE

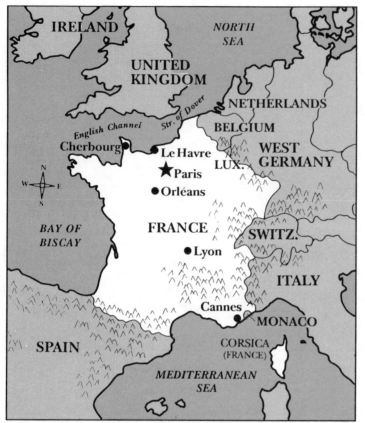

**Map Study:** *Is the city of Paris located on the coast of France or is it inland? What about Le Havre? Cannes? Orléans? Cherbourg? What body of water forms part of France's southern border? Name five countries that share France's eastern border.*

## France Has a Varied Geography

There are many different geographic areas in France. They range from lowlands in the north to the mountains in the west and south. Most of the land in this country is relatively flat. About two-thirds of France is less than 820 feet above sea level.

However, the land rises gradually as you move from northern France toward the south and west. The highest point in France is Mont Blanc, which is almost 16,000 feet high. It is part of the French Alps that form the border between France and Italy and Spain.

Sharing borders with so many other nations has shaped French culture. For example, many regions in eastern France have been controlled by both Germany and France at different times in their history. The people in these regions often speak German, and observe many traditions of the German culture.

## France Has a Varied Climate

France's climate is just as varied as its geography. Generally, the climate of French regions is determined by the region's distance from the ocean. Regions of France that are near the Atlantic Ocean have a rainy climate. Their winters are mild; their summers are cool. Regions of France that are near the Mediterranean Sea have a warmer, drier climate.

As you move away from the coast, the French climate changes. Winters are colder, and summers are hotter. The mountainous areas of France get a great deal of snow during the winter.

## The French Enjoy These Climate Differences

French farmers take advantage of these different climates to raise many products, including beef and other kinds of cattle. France is one of the leading agricultural countries in Europe. Milk from French cows, ewes, and goats is used to make over 300 types of cheese. The ideal climate in several French regions makes

*Cannes, on the French Riviera (Mediterranean Coast) is a popular resort. It is also the home of the world-famous Cannes Film Festival.*

France one of the leading producers of the world's wines.

The French take advantage of these climate differences. They can visit resorts on the Mediterranean coast for summer sports, or travel to resorts in the mountains for many winter sports.

**R E V I E W**

**Directions:**
Number your paper from 1 to 5. Answer the following questions.
1. Why do many French people call France "L'hexagon"?
2. France has no natural boundary markers with Germany. How has this influenced French history?
3. Name three of the countries that share a border with France.
4. How is the climate in the Atlantic coastal regions of France different from the climate in the regions of France that border the Mediterranean Sea?
5. How has France's climate made it one of the leading agricultural countries in Europe?

# SPOTLIGHT
## S T O R Y

## The Caves at Lascaux

In 1940, a small French boy and his dog were running through the fields near Lascaux, in southwestern France. Suddenly, the dog disappeared into a large hole. The boy climbed into the hole to retrieve his dog. He could not believe what he found.

In the dim light of the cave, the boy saw that the walls of the cavern were covered with drawings. There were pictures of bulls, horses, ibexes, and wildcats.

This young French boy had made a very important discovery. The cave is one of many found in the southwestern part of France. It contains the best examples of prehistoric French art. Scientists estimate that people living in France over 30,000 years ago made the drawings. They used powdered minerals mixed with animal fat to create the blacks, reds, browns, and yellows of the pictures. Many think these caves may have been used for religious purposes. There are few pictures of man among the numerous drawings.

The caves at Lascaux were first opened to the public in 1948, but the effects of this were soon seen. The outside air and the carbon dioxide exhaled by the visitors were ruining the pictures. The caves were closed to the public in 1963. Today, people can visit models of the caves, and enjoy this earliest form of French art.

**Stop and Review**
Write the answers to these questions on your paper.
1. How were the caves at Lascaux first discovered?
2. Why was this an important discovery?
3. Who do scientists think made the drawings? Why did they make them?
4. What do you think could be some other possible explanations for why the drawings were made?
5. Why were the caves closed to the public in 1963?

*Pictures of animals cover the walls inside the caves at Lascaux.*

# PART 2:
# History of France

**P**eople have been living in the area we now call France for thousands of years. *Archaeologists* have found early evidence of these people, particularly in southern France. You can still visit models of the caves where these early inhabitants recorded their exploits.

**The Celts Come to France**

The Celts were one of the first tribes to invade France and the first to actually farm in the region. They were organized into many small tribes. The most powerful tribe was called the *Gallia*. The Celts soon had to defend their land from the Roman Empire. The Romans had taken over many areas surrounding the land controlled by the Celtic tribes. They called this land Gaul. They wanted to add Gaul to their growing empire. The Celts united to fight the invading armies, but under Julius Caesar, Roman soldiers defeated them. In 52 B.C., Gaul became a province of the Roman Empire.

**Germanic Tribes Invade France**

Gaul grew and prospered as part of the Roman Empire for the next

*During the Dark Ages, people in France began building castles to protect themselves from the invading Germanic tribes.*

400 years. However, as Rome grew weak, tribes from Germany began to attack and conquer parts of their territory. When these tribes attacked Rome, the emperor ordered Roman soldiers back to the city to defend the heart of the empire. Gaul lost the protection of the Roman army. German tribes swept into Gaul and soon conquered the area. This was the start of a time period in Europe called the *Dark Ages*. Europeans turned their attention away from the arts and from learning. They had to

fight for their own survival. The Dark Ages correspond roughly to the time known as the Middle Ages.

## The Franks Gain Control of Gaul

France gradually became known as the land of the *Franks*. The Franks were a powerful tribe that came from the area we now call Germany. Charlemagne was an important leader of the Franks. In French, his name means "Charles the Great." Under his leadership, the territory controlled by the Franks grew and grew. By the 800s, Charlemagne's armies had conquered most of Western Europe. When Charlemagne died, his empire was divided into three separate kingdoms. Each kingdom was controlled by one of Charlemagne's grandsons. None of them could ever match the power or wisdom of Charlemagne. This division led to many modern day struggles between the western kingdom, France, and the eastern kingdom, Germany.

## The Normans Involve France with England

In the 900s, Vikings from Scandinavia began to invade and take over areas in the eastern part of present-day France. These Vikings were sometimes called Norsemen. In France, they became *Normans*, and lived in the area of France we call Normandy. In the 1000s, these Normans struck out against the English. The Norman leader William conquered the English army at the Battle of Hastings in 1066. For many years, Norman kings ruled England.

## The Hundred Years' War

The Normans intermarried with the English, and their control extended to areas of France. Many French people were upset that people of English birth were now in control of French territory. This led to a conflict that lasted over one hundred years. Today, we call it the *Hundred Years' War*. It began in 1337, when the English king Edward III invaded French territory. The only thing that stopped the fighting was the Black Plague, which raged through Europe in the 1300s.

The spirit of a young girl helped bring an end to this war. Her name was Joan of Arc. She led a group of French to victory over the English at Orléans in 1429. Although she was later tried and burned as a witch, her courage lived on. The French finally drove the English out of France in 1453.

## Joan of Arc

Joan of Arc was a simple peasant girl who lived in France during the early 1400s. At the time, her country was involved in a great struggle with England. When she was only 17, Joan began to have visions. She saw herself leading the French army to victory over the English.

Joan approached the young king of France and told him of her mission from God. He became convinced of her sincerity, and gave her the command of the king's troops. Up to that point, the English had won every battle. Joan changed that. In 1429, French soldiers led by Joan liberated the city of Orléans. Four other victories quickly followed. Joan felt that she had done all she could for France, but the king begged her to stay on. Dismayed, she fought on. Finally, French allies of the English captured Joan and sold her to the English for about $3,000. The English accused her of being a witch, tried her, and finally burned her at the stake.

Joan of Arc still lives on in the memory of the French, and in the minds of people everywhere who fight for their freedom. She was made a saint by the Catholic Church in 1920.

### The Reformation in France

During the 1500s, the *Reformation* began in Europe. Many French people became Protestants. They were called *Huguenots*. The French government was controlled by Catholics. They persecuted the Huguenots, killing thousands of them. Finally, a Huguenot king, Henry IV, became King of France. He had to convert to Catholicism before he was crowned. But he never forgot his past. Soon after he became king, Henry signed the *Edict of Nantes*, giving French people the freedom to worship as they pleased.

### The Sun King

For many years, the French king and the noble class fought for control of the national government. The kings had been able to keep most of the power in their hands. King Louis XIV was perhaps the most successful. He built a grand palace at Versailles. He forced all the nobles to move into homes surrounding his palace. Through this and other actions, he made the power of the king absolute. This king chose the noble sun as a symbol of his rule.

### The French Revolution

The French people grew discontent with the state of their government. They had to pay steep taxes to support the richest people in the land: the kings, the church, and the nobles. They had also seen the American colonies win their freedom from the English. They decided it was their turn.

# FRANCE

On July 14, 1789, the people stormed the *Bastille*, a French prison in Paris. They slaughtered the guards and captured the prison on behalf of the people. The revolution for French freedom had begun. Ten years later, the people had won. They set up the first French *republic*.

## Napoleon's Rise to Power

The first republic did not last very long. In 1799, Napoleon and the men he led seized control of the government. Gradually, he took more and more power away from others in government. Finally, in 1804, Napoleon crowned himself Emperor of France. He then turned his armies against the rest of Europe, quickly expanding his empire.

*Did you know that the Eiffel Tower in Paris was used as a military observation tower during World War I?*

*Napoleon began building the Arc de Triomphe (Arch of Triumph) in 1806 to honor his soldiers. Listed on the inside wall of the Arc are the names of 386 of his soldiers and 96 of his own triumphs.*

Napoleon was finally defeated at the Battle of Waterloo in 1815. He was exiled to live the rest of his life on the island of St. Helena, off the west coast of Africa.

## The Wars with Germany

Beginning in the 1800s, France's history was tied to Germany. The region of Prussia led a newly unified Germany. In 1870, Prussia invaded France. Prussia defeated the French, and they were forced to give Alsace and parts of Lorraine to Prussia. These two regions are near the German-French border.

In World War I, German troops again invaded France. This time, France, with the help of its Allies, was the victor. In the treaty that ended the war, France was given back the land it had lost. But the French wanted to punish the Germans. They forced Germany to pay *reparations* for the damage Germans had done to their land.

After the war, France tried to protect itself from another invasion. It built the *Maginot Line*, a series of defenses on the French-German border. However, this did not stop the Germans. Under Hitler's direction, German troops bypassed the Maginot Line and invaded France in 1940. Germany took over two-thirds of French territory. They allowed the French to set up a government in the south of France. However, it was a puppet government. Germany actually controlled it. Some French fought to reestablish their country. They were called the Resistance. Again, with the help of the Allies, they were successful.

## France Today

France worked hard to recover from the war, aided by support and money from the American government. It has since emerged as a great industrial and agricultural power. The government of France today is led by members of France's *Socialist* Party. For the first time since 1947, Communist Party members serve in the French Cabinet.

| R E V I E W | **Directions:** |
|---|---|
| | Number your paper from 1 to 5. Answer the following questions. |
| | 1. What did the fall of the Roman Empire mean to the French? |
| | 2. What part of Charlemagne's empire became modern-day France? |
| | 3. Who were the Huguenots? |
| | 4. What was one factor that led to the French Revolution? |
| | 5. Give one example of the way Germany influenced modern French history. |

# FRANCE

## PART 3:
## Language and the Arts

People in France speak French. It is a Romance language, based on Latin. Other languages are spoken in some parts of the country. For example, the people in Brittany, on the Atlantic coast of France, often speak *Breton*. Breton is a type of Celtic language, like Welsh and Gaelic.

The French are very proud of their language. There is a special group of French intellectuals that was set up to preserve the country's language traditions. This group is called the Académie Francaise. They work today to keep the French language from adopting terms from other languages.

### French Is a World Language

Many other countries also use French as their official language. These include Belgium, Monaco, and Switzerland. French is also a language that is used by diplomats around the world. Today, it is an official language of the United Nations.

### French Literature

Over the centuries, French authors have written some of the most influential literature in the world. Famous writers such as Francois Rabelais and Victor Hugo have written great fiction that is still read today. French dramatists such as Molière created plays during the French Renaissance that are produced and enjoyed today.

Most French writers have concentrated on the principle of *rationalism* in their writing. Rationalism concentrates on the reasons behind human actions. It also emphasizes clear, concise writing.

| Some French Words | | |
|---|---|---|
| **English** | **French** | **Pronunciation** |
| please | s'il vous plait | seel´-voh-pleh |
| yes | oui | wee |
| good evening | bon soir | bawn-swahr´ |

## French Artists

France has always had a special bond with the arts. At one time, Paris was considered the art capital of the world. Many famous artists lived and worked in this ancient city. They often developed a distinct style, or school, of painting. One of the most famous of these schools was the Impressionist school. French artists such as Edouard Manet, Claude Monet, and Pierre Auguste Renoir painted in this style. The impressionist tradition was carried on by Paul Cézanne and Paul Gauguin.

*The Louvre in Paris is one of the largest art museums in the world. More than 275,000 works of art are displayed in the museum's 140 exhibition rooms and 8 miles of galleries. The Louvre contains many works by French artists, as well as important paintings from other European masters, such as Leonardo da Vinci's* Mona Lisa.

---

**R E V I E W**

**Directions:**
Number your paper from 1 to 5. Answer the following questions.
1. Why was the Académie Francais set up?
2. Name a language, aside from French, that is spoken in France today.
3. Name two countries, besides France, that use French as an official language.
4. What is rationalism?
5. Name one school of painting that was developed by French artists.

# FRANCE

## PART 4:
## Life in Modern France

The basic money unit of France is the *franc*. There are 100 *centimes* in a franc. In 1989, the American dollar was worth about six francs.

The French enjoy a high *standard of living*. This means that there are a great deal of consumer goods available, and salaries are high enough for people to be able to afford to buy what they need and want.

France is both a great industrial power and a leading agricultural nation. About 30 percent of the French earn their living by working in the many industries that have grown up in France since the end of World War II. Only 5 percent of

*The French enjoy skiing and other winter sports in their country's mountains.*

the French work in agriculture. However, modern farming techniques have made France the leading producer of agricultural goods in the EEC. The EEC (European Economic Community) is a group of European nations united to promote their economic well-being.

### Entertainment

Like most Europeans, the French love soccer. They call it *le foot*. They also enjoy skiing and other winter sports in the mountains of France, as well as the delights offered by French resorts on the Mediterranean coast. Most French families have the time to enjoy a real vacation. French workers are guaranteed by law at least a month of vacation time a year. They usually take this time in August.

*French vineyards produce some of the world's finest wines.*

*Bicycling is a popular pastime in France. While some cyclists compete for sport, others prefer to relax and enjoy the scenery as they peddle through the countryside.*

Not everyone in France owns a car, but probably everyone has a bicycle. The French have elevated bicycling to a national sport. Every year, they sponsor a championship bicycle race called the *Tour de France.* Participants travel throughout France, ending up in Paris. The winner of the Tour is a national hero.

Most French cities and towns have at least one outdoor café. People love to pass their time at the café, sipping coffee or a small glass of wine, and watching people stroll by. This is a long-standing tradition in France.

The first cafés were opened in the 1600s, long before the United States was even formed.

## Paris

Paris is more than just the French capital. It is also the largest city in France and one of the oldest, as well. People have lived in Paris for over two thousand years. But Paris is also a modern city. Almost nine million people live in the city and the suburbs that surround it.

Paris is filled with the grandeur of past and present-day France. Within the city, you can find ancient buildings of great importance to French history. One of these is the Conciergerie. This used to be the king's attendant's home. During the French Revolution, it was used to hold prisoners before they were guillotined. Some of the ancient buildings have been converted to other uses. For example, the Louvre was built as a fortified castle. Today, it is a famous museum.

Parisians can enjoy some of the world's best restaurants and the finest entertainments, and buy their clothes at the houses of international designers. Or they can sit at an outdoor café for hours at a time, letting their eyes explore the beauty of Paris.

*The Champs Elysées is one of the busiest promenades in Paris.*

# FRANCE

## Celebrations

Many French holidays celebrate events that are part of the country's history. Le Huit Mai, or the Eighth of May, is a day that is celebrated to mark the end of World War II. The French place wreaths on the graves of those killed in the war on this day. The end of World War I is marked by Le Onze Novembre. This means the Eleventh of November. On this day, the French signed an armistice agreement with Germany. On July 14, the French celebrate La Fete Nationale. This is the day the French commemorate the storming of the Bastille prison in Paris. This act was the start of the French Revolution.

We do not celebrate these French holidays, but there are similar holidays that celebrate events that are part of American history. Can you name them?

## Religion

France does not have an official religion. But most French people belong to the Roman Catholic Church. About two percent of the French belong to the Protestant religion.

Most of the national holidays in France have Catholic roots. For example, Ascension Thursday is a legal holiday. This is the day that Catholics celebrate the ascent of Christ into heaven.

Most French Catholics observe a time before Easter that is called Lent. It is a time of preparation for this special holiday. During Lent, many people try to do good works and not eat as much as they normally would. But, before Lent, the French celebrate. Lent begins on Ash Wednesday. The Tuesday before this is called

*Breton women often wear this traditional costume, with its high, starched coiffe (headdress), on special holidays in the region.*

Mardi Gras, which means Fat Tuesday in French. Mardi Gras combines the traditions from France's ancient past with the customs of their religion. Towns throughout France have a carnival on this day, with a special parade. The parade features flower-covered floats and huge cardboard figures. At the end of the day, the people of the town gather and burn a figure they call *Carnaval.* This is a huge, grotesque doll. It is supposed to represent all the evil in the world. In this country, we have a similar tradition that is held each year in New Orleans. It was brought to our country by the French people who settled in this region.

### Education

French students must attend school from the ages of six to sixteen. Most of them go to public schools supported by the government. About 20 percent attend private schools. Most of these schools are run by the Catholic Church.

French children attend elementary school until they are 13. Boys and girls usually do not go to the same school. After high school, French students must pass a national test before they are allowed to study at a French university.

### The Family

The family is very important to French people. In the recent past, it was not unusual to find two or three generations of the family living in one home. Today, this is no longer true. However, most people do not move far from where their family lives, and enjoy getting together with other family members as often as possible.

Just as American families do, the French have special days to honor their parents. They celebrate La Fete des Meres on the last Sunday of May, in honor of their mothers. La Fete des Peres honors all French fathers. It is observed on the third Sunday in June.

Many French soldiers lost their lives during the world wars of this century. Some French women have felt that it was their duty to the state to have children. The government supports this idea by paying flat-rate family allowances to families for every child they have, after the first.

### French Cuisine

The French have turned cooking into a fine art. French cuisine is world-renowned. The techniques and recipes that the French have created are used by cooks throughout the world. In the United States, many of the cooking terms we use today, such as "sauté" or "au gratin" are actually French words for cooking techniques. "Gourmet" is also a French word, and rightfully so.

France has a long history of fine cooking — and eating. The Romans who occupied their land were supposedly shocked by how much the Gauls ate. Nevertheless, they soon grew to love many foods the Gauls prepared, such as snails and foie gras, which is a paste made of liver.

The French say that their first great gourmet was Charlemagne. When holidays came, Charlemagne invited many people to enjoy a special feast, even the ladies. This was scandalous at the time. Ladies did not usually eat with men. Charlemagne and his guests feasted on whole roasted animals and delicacies such as peacock pie.

In 1553, the first public eating houses were opened in Paris. If you would have visited one, you would have been able to order specialties such as minced dormouse and porpoise pie, or even ice cream.

The French Revolution also had its effect on the culinary traditions of France. Many of the noble people in France were killed during the revolution. The people who worked for them, including their chefs, no longer had jobs. In order to support themselves, these cooks opened cafés and restaurants throughout the country. Some of these old cafés are still in business today.

The French enjoy the fruits of their land and the sea that surrounds them. Each area of France has special dishes that chefs in that region prepare, based on the foods that are available to them. Lorraine is known for quiche lorraine, a cheese custard pie. Crepes are popular in Brittany. Crepes are very flat pancakes that are served with sugar or jam. Boeuf bourguignonne is a beef stew prepared in the Burgundy region. And if you had a taste for seafood stew, you'd probably want to visit Provence, a region known for its bouillabaisse.

Eating on the run also has a place in modern-day France. In Paris today you can find many of the same fast-food restaurants that you and your friends visit each day. But, the French are still, after all, French. They have not forgotten their tradition of fine cuisine. The latest craze in fast food is the French-prepared Panka. Panka is frozen beef bourguignonne or chicken curry encased in bread. It is sold in vending machines throughout the country.

## Shopping for Food in France

French families have to shop for food, just like families everywhere. They can choose to visit a supermarket that looks very much like the one where your family goes. But, many French people still prefer to shop at the small specialty stores that are in every town. They will buy their meat from a butcher, who will cut it especially for them. If they want horse meat, they have to go to a special shop that sells only horse meat. You can tell these shops by the figure of a horse they have outside them. If they want pastry or cakes, they will go to one special shop; if they want to buy bread, they will go to another.

Americans usually shop for the week. Most French people would not think of doing this. Every day, a family member will visit the supermarket or specialty shops to purchase the food the family will use that day.

*A grandfather and his grandson bicycle home after stopping for two baguettes (French bread).*

Their refrigerators are not as large as the one you have in your home, and cannot hold as much food.

**REVIEW**

**Directions:**
Number your paper from 1 to 5. Answer the following questions.
1. What is the basic money unit of France?
2. What is "le foot"?
3. Give one example of the way that Roman Catholicism has influenced French culture.
4. What are some French holidays that are similar to holidays observed in the United States?
5. Why is it a better choice to call French cooking "cuisine"?

# FRANCE

## MAP SKILLS

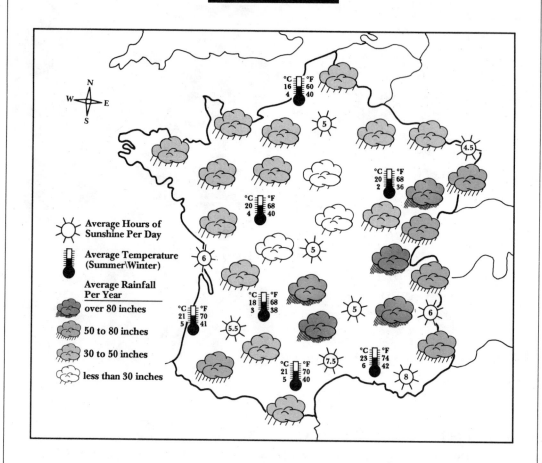

# TEMPERATURE AND RAINFALL MAP OF FRANCE

This map uses different symbols to show information about temperature and rainfall. Look at the map legend to find out what these symbols mean.

**Directions:** Using the map above, answer the following questions about France's climate.

1. What symbol does this map use for average temperature?
2. In what part of France (North, South, East, or West) is the average daily temperature the highest?
3. What is the lowest average rainfall per year?
4. In what part of the country does the lowest average rainfall occur?
5. In what part of France are there more hours of sunshine?
6. What is the least number of hours of sun per day on this map? What is the most hours of sun per day?

# CHAPTER 5 REVIEW

## Summary of France

*The culture that has developed in this, the largest country in Western Europe, stretches back thousands of years. Modern-day life in "L'hexagon" owes a great deal to the influences of a varied geography, climate, and history. One geographic feature that has strongly affected modern French culture is the lack of protection from a natural boundary marker on France's border with Germany.*

*Celtic, Germanic, and Roman cultures have all contributed to French culture, as people from these countries invaded this land. Strong leaders such as Charlemagne, Louis XIV, and Napoleon have steered this nation to a position of world importance that still exists today.*

*Life in modern France continues a tradition of appreciation for the arts, especially the art of preparing and cooking delicious foods. The French also have a high standard of living that allows them time to enjoy family life, a very important part of their culture. Sports such as "le foot" (soccer) and bicycling are popular as well.*

## Critical Thinking Skills

**Directions:** Give some serious thought to the questions below. Be sure to answer in complete sentences.

1. How do the various geographic forms of France influence the climate of the different regions of France?
2. Give one example of the way French history would be changed if there had been a mountain range between France and Germany.
3. Do you feel that France would have defeated the Germans during World Wars I and II without the help of the Allies? Defend your opinion.
4. Give one reason why French is used as a language of diplomats.

5. Why do many countries use so many French words for cooking?

## For Discussion

**Directions:** Discuss these questions with your class. Appoint one class member to write the ideas you discover on the board.

1. Do you feel it was right for the French government to persecute the Huguenots? In general, is there ever a time when it is morally correct for a government to try to control a religious group?
2. Do you think a nation should be forced to pay reparations for damages they caused during a war? Should only the country who lost pay, or should all the countries who were involved in the war?
3. What are some of the reasons that the French government gives its families an allowance for every child they have after the first? Do you think this policy would work in the United States?

## Write It!

**Directions:** Look up the meaning of these French terms in a dictionary: *sauté, cuisine,* and *gourmet*. Write a simple definition for each word, then use each one in a sentence.

## For You to Do

**Directions:** Paris is one of the most beautiful cities in the world. Visit your school or local library and find a book about touring Paris. As a class, make a list of all the attractions in the city. Have it duplicated so that each class member can have a copy. Ask students to check off the attractions they would most like to visit. Analyze the information by comparing all the lists. Which places would most people like to visit? Which were not very popular?

# EAST AND WEST GERMANY

| | |
|---|---|
| **F A C T S** | • East and West Germany are located in the center of Western Europe.<br>• West Germany is a federal republic closely tied to the West.<br>• East Germany is a Communist country closely allied to the Soviet Union.<br>• West Germany's capital is Bonn. East Germany's capital is East Berlin.<br>• West Germany is one of the world's most densely-populated countries. |

## PART 1:
## Geography and Climate of Germany

East and West Germany are located in the center of Europe. There are no natural boundary markers on their eastern and western borders. Natural boundary markers include features such as mountains or seas. Both countries border on many other European nations. This proximity to other countries has figured greatly into German culture through the centuries. Germans could easily move into other areas of Europe. Trading with distant neighbors was relatively easy. Traditions of German culture were passed to other nations. The German travelers adopted some traditions of the people they met.

In times of war, German armies have taken advantage of this ready access to other European countries. It was easy for them to march into other nations and conquer them.

# EAST AND WEST GERMANY

**Map Study:** *Is the city of East Berlin located in East Germany or West Germany? What about Munich? Dresden? Oberammergau? Hamburg? Bonn? Which country is more mountainous — East or West Germany? What country shares East Germany's eastern border?*

## Germany Has Many Different Kinds of Geographic Regions

Germany stretches from the *North Sea* in the north, to the *Bavarian Alps* in the south.

The area from the North Sea southward is a level plain that is almost flat. This is the largest land form in Germany. The southern part of the plain has very fertile soil. Most of German farming takes place in this area. Many Germans live in this geographic region.

The land gradually slopes upward as you move away from the plain. Near the German border with Switzerland, the land rises abruptly in the Bavarian Alps. These mountains are part of the largest mountain system in Europe. Some of the mountains in the Bavarian Alps are over 8,000 feet high.

The Black Forest, or Schwarzwald in German, is located in the southern part of West Germany. It became known as the Black Forest because the trees in this area grew so close together that they looked black. This forest is featured in many German legends and fairy tales.

## The Rhine River Is an Important German River

Some people have described the Rhine River as the most important river in Europe. It begins in Switzerland and travels through Germany and The Netherlands before it ends in the North Sea. The Rhine is very important to the development of German culture. Stories about many

## The Lorelei

Many German folk tales are set in the beautiful valley that surrounds the Rhine River. One story involves the river itself.

Where the river widens out south of the Bingen, its waters become very dangerous to sailors. The Lorelei is a high cliff at the river's edge. Sometimes, you can hear a mournful sound in this part of the river. It is probably due to sounds echoing off the high walls of the cliff.

However, German legend says it is the voice of a wicked water fairy. They say she sits on the cliff, singing to the sailors that pass by. She hopes that her beautiful voice will lure them toward the shore, where they will wreck their boats.

Many German authors have written about the deadly charms of the Lorelei and her haunting voice.

ancient German heroes are set in the Rhine Valley region. Many large German cities, such as Cologne (Köln) and Bonn, are located on the Rhine's banks.

### Germany's Climate Is Varied

Germany's climate is influenced by the west winds that blow across the two countries. They bring warm weather in the winter and moderate temperatures in the summer. In the winter, the average temperature throughout these countries is about 30° Fahrenheit. In the summer, the average temperature is about 70° Fahrenheit.

However, the weather can be more extreme in the southern and eastern parts of Germany.

### Germany Receives a Moderate Amount of Rainfall

Most of Germany receives between 20 and 40 inches of *precipitation* during the year. In the western regions of Germany, the rain falls moderately throughout the year. In the eastern parts of Germany, the rain comes mostly during the summer, in the form of heavy downpours during thunderstorms.

During the winter, the mountainous regions of Germany receive the most snowfall. Some of the higher peaks are snow-covered throughout the year. Many Germans enjoy skiing and other winter sports in these areas of Germany.

*A German family enjoys the snowy countryside of the Bavarian Alps from a horse-drawn sleigh.*

# EAST AND WEST GERMANY

**R E V I E W**

**Directions:**
Number your paper from 1 to 5. Answer the following questions.
1. Germany is at the center of Europe. Name one way that this has affected German culture.
2. What is the largest land area in Germany?
3. What body of water forms the northern border of West Germany?
4. Where are the Bavarian Alps located?
5. How would you describe Germany's climate?

## PART 2:
## History of Germany

Germany was not a truly united country until the 1870s. In early times, German tribes controlled different regions of the country.

The early German tribes are often described as warlike. They were excellent soldiers and used their skills to keep control of their lands. These tribes included the Franks, the Goths, the Vandals, the Germani, and the Cimbri.

Eventually, these German tribes swept into Rome and conquered the Romans. They divided the Roman Empire into smaller kingdoms. Each kingdom was controlled by a different tribe.

### The Kingdom of the Franks

The kingdom controlled by the Franks soon became very powerful. It started in the land we now call France. Charlemagne became the leader of this kingdom. His name means "Charles the Great," an appropriate name for this important leader. He unified a large area of Western Europe under his control.

Charlemagne's empire was divided in the year 843 into eastern, middle, and western kingdoms. Charlemagne's grandsons were chosen to lead each kingdom.

### The Holy Roman Empire Begins

Gradually, separate regions in the German kingdoms, called *duchies*, grew powerful. A duchy is an area under the control of a duke. Saxony was one of the most important duchies. Saxon kings were to lead Germany for the next 1,000 years.

In 962, the Saxon leader Otto I became the Emperor of Germany.

The Holy Roman Empire had begun. It soon became the best organized, most powerful country in Europe.

During the many years of the Holy Roman Empire, cities along the Rhine grew in importance. As the empire weakened, the cities became even more powerful. They formed *leagues* to consolidate their strength. One of the most important was the *Hanseatic League*, formed in the late 1200s.

*Serfdom* became an accepted practice in the Holy Roman Empire. Noblemen would force poor people to be their slaves, or serfs. This practice continued in the western part of the empire until the 1800s.

Like most of Europe, Germany was ravaged by the Black Death in the Middle Ages. Many people were killed by this incurable disease. The destruction caused by this epidemic greatly affected German culture.

## The Oberammergau Passion Play

In the 1600s, the bubonic plague swept through Europe. This disease was also called the Black Death. It was spread by poor sanitary conditions. Once a person contracted the plague, there was nothing anyone could do. Within a short time, the person would die. The Black Death killed thousands. Everyone lived in fear of becoming ill and tried to do anything they could to avoid contracting the plague.

The residents of Oberammergau, Germany, prayed daily that the plague would not come to their town. They promised that if God spared their town from this terrible disease, they would perform a special play every ten years. It would be a play about the life and death of Jesus. This type of play is called a passion play.

The plague never came to Oberammergau. The people were so grateful that they started performing the play. The first passion play was held in 1634. The tradition has continued over the years. Today, people from all over the world come to Bavaria to see the Oberammergau Passion Play.

*The charming town of Rothenburg ob der Tauber is a typical German medieval town.*

In 1517, the *Reformation* began in Germany. This was a movement by groups of religious leaders who were upset with many doctrines and practices of the Roman Catholic Church. These people became known as Protestants, because they protested against the Church. One of the leaders of the movement was Martin

*The Brandenburg Gate was built in 1791. Today, it is Berlin's most famous landmark. It stands just inside the Berlin Wall in East Germany. People used to travel through this gate to go from East Germany to West Germany.*

Luther. By 1555, the German government officially recognized the Lutheran Church that Luther started.

## Prussia Rises to Lead Germany

Prussia was a state in the north central part of Germany. This state had an excellent army that brought more and more territory under Prussian control. Soon, Prussia covered most of East Germany, parts of Poland, and sections of the Soviet Union.

By 1806, the French leader Napoleon had taken over parts of Germany. In 1815, Prussia joined Great Britain, Russia, and Austria in defeat-ing him during the Battle of Waterloo. In the treaty that settled this conflict, Prussia was given even more land.

By the 1870s, Prussia's power was almost absolute. They had formed a *confederation* of northern German states. Finally, states in southern Germany joined them. On January 18, 1871, the Prussian leader Wilhelm I was crowned *kaiser* of the unified German Empire. "Kaiser" means "emperor."

Under Prussian leadership, Germany entered World War I. With Austria-Hungary and other friendly nations, they fought against the *Allies*. The United States entered the war in 1917. Germany's fate was sealed. The Germans signed an *armistice* on November 11, 1918. The official treaty that ended the war was called the *Treaty of Versailles*. The treaty disarmed Germany and forced it to give up certain lands. It also demanded that the German government pay *reparations* to other countries to make up for the damage they caused during the war.

### Hitler Comes to Power

After the war, Germans forced their Prussian leaders out of the country and established the *Weimar Republic*. It was on shaky ground from the very start. The German economy was in shambles. Many Germans did not want the republic. Some wanted a Communist form of government. Others wanted the Emperor to return.

In this political confusion, one man and one political party arose. His name was Adolf Hitler, and his party was known as the *Nazis*. This was an abbreviated form of the National Socialist German Workers' Party.

Hitler's dream of a pure German empire led to some of the worst atrocities ever known to man. Six million Jews, and countless others, were killed in concentration camps and elsewhere. Hitler wanted to get rid of people whom he considered to have "impure," non-Germanic blood.

Hitler's dream also led to the nightmare of World War II. Hitler attacked neighboring nations. He made them part of his *Third Reich*. This unprovoked aggression led the Allies to declare war on Germany. Towards the end of World War II, Hitler knew his dream was dying. He committed suicide. Germany surrendered to the Allies.

*Soviet soldiers at the war-torn Brandenburg Gate. The Soviet Army helped the Allies defeat the Nazis in May of 1945.*

# EAST AND WEST GERMANY

# SPOTLIGHT
# S T O R Y

## The Berlin Wall

Germany was defeated in World War II. The Allies — France, Great Britain, Russia, and the United States — divided the German territory among themselves.

The old capital of Germany was Berlin. The Allies divided this city into western and eastern parts. Berlin was deep in the territory that was controlled by the Russians.

After the war, tensions between the old Allies grew. This was known as the Cold War. There were no battles during this war; it involved a conflict of ideas about the best way to run a country. The Russians believed in communism. The Western nations believed in representative forms of democracy. The Russians became suspicious of the other three countries. They wanted Berlin to be all theirs. The other three Allies wanted to reunite Germany. Russia did not want to lose control of its part of Germany.

First, in 1948, the Russians blockaded Berlin. No one could travel through East Germany to reach Berlin. The Russians thought this would force the other three countries out of Berlin. Instead, Britain, France, and the United States started an airlift to bring food and other supplies to the people living in West Berlin. The Russians had to stop their blockade.

Many people in East Germany were not happy with the Communist government. Weekly, many escaped from East to West Berlin. In response, the East German government built a heavily fortified wall dividing the two sectors of Berlin. Their soldiers shot anyone who tried to go to West Berlin.

In 1989, many people tried to leave East Germany. However, this time their government reacted differently. On November 9, 1989, government officials said that all East Germans could travel freely to the West.

The Berlin Wall was once a symbol of the division between communism and democracy. Now it is little more than a broken wall.

**Stop and Review**
Write the answers to these questions on your paper.
1. What were the four countries that controlled Berlin after World War II?
2. What was the Cold War?
3. How did Russia try to control travel to Berlin?
4. What did East Germany do to keep people from leaving East Berlin?
5. In 1989, how did East Germany change its travel policy?
6. What did the Berlin Wall symbolize? How has this changed since 1989?

*People entering or leaving West Berlin must pass through special checkpoints where their official papers are checked by both East German soldiers and Allied troops.*

**A Divided Germany**

At the end of the war, the Allies occupied Germany. France, Great Britain, the United States, and Russia were each given sectors of the country. The city of Berlin was also divided between the four. This division of Germany still continues to this day.

France, Great Britain, and the United States each controlled part of West Germany. The Russian sector was in East Germany. As tensions between these two factions increased, the chances for reuniting Germany decreased.

Although the Allies have long left Germany, East and West Germany bear their marks. East Germany, now known as the German Democratic Republic, is closely allied with the Soviet Union. Its government is modeled on the Russian government. West Germany is more closely associated with Western Europe and the United States.

R
E
V
I
E
W

**Directions:**
Number your paper from 1 to 6. Answer the following questions.
1.  Name three of the tribes that controlled German lands during ancient times.
2.  What is Saxony? What effect did it have on German history?
3.  How did Prussia become so powerful?
4.  What were two provisions of the Treaty of Versailles?
5.  How did Hitler's actions provoke World War II?
6.  How were East and West Germany formed?

# EAST AND WEST GERMANY

## PART 3:
## Language, the Arts, and Inventions

The official language of both East and West Germany is German. German is also the official language of Austria and the tiny kingdom of Liechtenstein. In addition, German is one of the official languages of Switzerland and Luxembourg. Altogether, over 120 million people speak German.

The German language and the English you speak are actually related to each other. They are both part of the Germanic family of languages. Some of the words are the same in both languages. For example, the German word for "hand" is "Hand," the same as it is for English. (German nouns are always capitalized.) Many words sound about the same in both languages, even though they are spelled differently. In English, we say "house," which is pronounced "hows." In German, it is spelled "Haus," but the word is pronounced "hows."

### The German Language Has Many Different Forms

In the past, there were two basic divisions of the German language. One was called *High German*, or Hochdeutsch. It is spoken in the "higher" regions of Germany, such as Bavaria. The other division is called *Low German*, or Plattdeutsch. Low German is spoken in the northern, flatter parts of Germany. Each division has many different dialects.

| Some German Words | | |
|---|---|---|
| **English** | **German** | **Pronunciation** |
| yes | ja | yah |
| house | Haus | hows |
| good-bye | auf wiedersehen | auf vee´-dehr-zayn |
| expressway | Autobahn | ow´-toh-bahn |
| *Note: In German, all nouns are capitalized. | | |

Today, there is a third division of the language. It is called *Standard German.* This form of German is based on High German. It is used in schools, books, magazines, and in other forms of public communication.

**Germans and Their Music**

Most experts agree that Germany's contributions completely changed the world of music as we know it today. Many great German composers, including Ludwig von Beethoven and Johann Sebastian Bach, wrote and performed some of the most beautiful music ever heard. Artists such as Johannes Brahms and Felix Mendelssohn continued the tradition. Today, audiences around the world delight in the musical works of these composers.

Richard Wagner was also an important German composer. He wrote operas that glorified ancient Germany and her cultural traditions, and was Hitler's favorite composer.

There are many festivals in East and West Germany at which the music of these famous composers is played. Music lovers from around the world attend these to listen to several days' entertainment featuring their favorite composer.

*This conductor leads a brass band in playing some traditional German folk music.*

**German Literature**

Through the years, many German writers have made outstanding contributions to the world of literature. Johann Wolfgang von Goethe, Herman Hesse, and Thomas Mann are a few of the German authors whose works are enjoyed by many cultures all over the world.

Today, many writers in West Germany have written works that try to deal with the shame their nation feels over what happened during the years Adolph Hitler controlled Germany. The West Germans have a word to describe this feeling. It is called "Vergangenheitsbewaltigung." This means "coping with the past." By writing about the problems of the past, these writers hope to ensure that they do not happen again.

# EAST AND WEST GERMANY

*Dr. Werner Von Braun was one of the world's leading rocket scientists. He escaped Germany at the end of World War II and came to the United States. He was instrumental in developing launch rockets for America's space program.*

## German Philosophers

The principles of many German philosophers have greatly influenced Western thought. Some of these philosophers include Georg Wilhelm Hegel, Immanuel Kant, and Arthur Schopenhauer. Philosophy is the study of ideas and thinking. The theories discovered by these men are still studied at universities around the world.

## Germany's Contribution to Science and Technology

Germany has always been known as a center of European learning, especially for science and mathematics. We owe many modern advances to German scientists. For years, Germany led the world in the development and manufacture of many of the precision instruments scientists use.

During World War II, German scientists uncovered many principles of modern rocket technology. The Space Age is, to a large degree, the product of German inventiveness.

R
E
V
I
E
W

**Directions:**
Number your paper from 1 to 5. Answer the following questions.
1. Name two countries that use German as their official language.
2. What is the form of German used in German schools and newspapers today? Is it like High German or Low German?
3. Who was Richard Wagner?
4. In what field of the arts did Thomas Mann and Herman Hesse make their contributions?
5. How did German scientists shape the Space Age?

# PART 4:
## Life in Modern Germany

The basic money unit of West Germany is the *deutsche mark*, or DM. The DM is also the basic money unit of East Germany. The West German mark is worth a bit more on world money markets today.

Over one-third of West Germany's workers are employed in the country's manufacturing industries. West Germany is the fourth largest industrial nation in the world. It grew to this powerful position by rebuilding its economy after World War II. This recovery amazed the world. Many call it a modern-day miracle.

In East Germany, almost 41 percent of the working force has jobs in manufacturing. Most industry in East Germany is owned and controlled by the government. East Germany also had to rebuild its industry after the war. Its recovery has not been as rapid as West Germany's.

### Entertainment and Sports

Germans have always enjoyed outside sports. Many young people in both countries go hiking and backpacking throughout the countryside. Along the way, they stay in youth *hostels*. These are places where

**Map Study:** *This map shows West German ports and cities. On what body of water are the ports of Kiel and Lübeck located? Name two major cities in the southern part of West Germany. Name two major cities that are located on the Rhine River. Name two ports in northern West Germany. What major city is located south of the port of Bremerhaven?*

*Lower Saxonian farm houses today serve as attractive taverns or provide pleasant holiday accommodations for vacationing families.*

young people can stay for a small fee. In German, they are called Jugendherberge. Some of the Jugendherberge are located in very old historic buildings. They usually have two dormitories — one for the girls and one for the boys.

Germans were the first to invent gymnastics. There are many German clubs where athletes can practice their gymnastic skills. The Germans excel at this sport in world competitions.

Like all Europeans, the Germans love soccer. They call it *füssball*. Over 4 million people belong to German soccer clubs in West Germany alone. Each club has many teams. Both boys and girls play this popular sport. When they are younger, they often play on the same team. Older boys and girls have separate teams.

Many Germans also enjoy a wide variety of winter sports, including downhill and cross-country skiing. German athletes often win medals at the Olympics in these types of events.

**Going Places in Germany**

Like most people everywhere, the Germans love to travel. If they want to get away by car, they can travel on the autobahn. An autobahn is a major highway. There is no speed limit on most of the autobahn. If you're a slow driver, you'd better keep to the right! Germans design and produce well-engineered cars to

## Cars in Germany

Through the years, West Germany has become one of the three leading nations in car production. German cars are known for their engineering and reliability. Today, people all over the world drive Mercedes-Benz, Audis, BMWs (Bavarian Motor Works), and Volkswagens.

Building cars is an old tradition in Germany. In 1885, two German inventors built one of the first cars. Their names were Karl Benz and Gottlieb Daimler.

The Volkswagen Beetle is an example of fitting a car to the needs of the people. "Volkswagen" actually means "people's car." During World War II, Adolf Hitler wanted an inexpensive, reliable car produced. The lowly Beetle was the result. It was designed by Ferdinand Porsche. The "Bug" quickly became one of the most popular cars ever produced.

handle the demands of traveling at high speeds.

Even if you don't have a car, it is easy to get around in Germany. Both East and West Germany have efficient train systems that will bring you to most every place in the country.

If you want to travel by plane, you might choose to fly with the official West German airline, Lufthansa.

*The Sorbs, East Germany's only national minority, often wear their traditional costumes on holidays.*

Lufthansa flies to many cities in Germany and the rest of Europe. It also has flights to the United States.

**National Costumes**

Germany is one European nation where national costumes are still frequently worn, particularly in Bavaria. The men there wear *lederhosen*, which are leather shorts with broad suspenders. Women from Bavaria often wear *dirndl skirts*. These are full, colorful skirts with a wide waistband that is laced up.

**Education**

Germany was one of the first countries to set up a public education system for all children. This kind of system started in Prussia during the 1800s. Today in West Germany, the education systems are basically controlled by the individual states. This is the same kind of system that is used in the United States. West German children must attend school from age six to age fourteen. In East Germany, the central government controls the education systems throughout the country. All schools teach their students about communism. East German students must attend school from ages six through sixteen.

*A kindergarten class in East Germany*

Germany is the birthplace of *kindergarten*. In German, this means "children's garden." Germans were the first to establish these kinds of schools for their young children.

## Religion

In West Germany, most people are Christians. Over half of them belong to the Protestant faith. Many of these Protestants belong to the Lutheran Church. This is the church that Martin Luther founded. About 45 percent of West Germans are Roman Catholic.

In the past, the East German government has tried to discourage its citizens from belonging to formal religious groups. However, 80 percent of the East Germans belong to Protestant churches, and about 11 percent are Roman Catholic. Only 7 percent of the East Germans claim to be nonreligious.

## Celebrations

When you think about Christmas, you usually picture a big tree trimmed with lights and shiny ornaments. You smell the delightful aroma of cookies baking in the kitchen — cookies like Pfeffernusse and Springerle. In your mind, you hear the sweet voices of carolers singing "Silent Night" and "Oh, Tannenbaum." All these images come to us from traditions that are part of the German celebration of Christmas.

*People in traditional costumes come to an old village church in Bavaria on Christmas eve. Attending church services on this special night is part of the German celebration of Christmas.*

By far, Christmas is the biggest holiday of the year in Germany. And, as you would imagine, there is a great deal of preparation that must be made for the holiday feast.

Many towns have special marketplaces that are set up in the weeks before Christmas. They are called "Christkindlesmarkt," which means "The Christ Child's Market" in German. These markets have existed for many hundreds of

*Like most Europeans, many Germans do their food shopping at small corner stores that are within walking distance of their homes.*

years. If a German family needs anything to do with Christmas — from decorations to special foods — they can find it here. When the market opens, the town's children march through the streets, carrying lighted lanterns. One child is dressed as the Christ Child. Two others are dressed as angels. They invite all the people in the town to come to the market.

Christmas is actually a three-day celebration. On Christmas Eve, German families light their Christmas tree and open their presents to each other. The children also find several gifts from Saint Nicholas under the tree. Then, it's time to enjoy a special dinner, featuring a fish dish.

The family will also attend church services.

On Christmas Day, the family stays at home and enjoys a traditional German feast of roast goose and a special fruit-filled bread called Christstollen. On the second day of Christmas, the Germans visit their friends to share the spirit of the season with them.

### Eating

Many traditional German foods were developed at a time when most people did not have ways to keep food fresh. They featured preparations that would make the food edible for a long time. Some of these

*Germans and visitors alike enjoy many of the special foods of German culture, such as wurst, sold at stands like this one.*

pfeffer (rabbit stew) or Spatzele (noodles). And don't forget to save room for dessert! The Germans make a delicious Black Forest cherry cake called Schwarzwalder Kirschtorte.

You might become curious if you were to watch German people eat. The Germans cut up their food by holding their fork in the left hand and their knife in the right, just as you do. However, the Germans

foods are sauerkraut (preserved cabbage) and sauerbraten (pickled beef).

Germans eat more sausage (wurst) than any other kind of meat. Some people say that there are over 500 different kinds of German sausage. The frankfurter that we eat in the United States is a distant cousin of these sausages. It was named after the city of Frankfurt. Hamburger was also named after the city of Hamburg, but Americans eat much more of this kind of meat than Germans do.

If you were to sit down to a meal in Germany, some of the specialties you might sample would be Hasen-

## Bier!

Beer has been produced for centuries in many different cultures. But today the Germans have made beer production their own special custom.

Beer, or, in German, Bier, is a favorite beverage of many Germans. They drink it at their main, noon-time meal, and again when they eat supper in the evening. They even have a special type of restaurant, called a bierkeller, where beer is served, along with sausages or spare ribs, and of course, sauerkraut.

There are many different types of German beer. Some of it is dark and bitter. Other brands are lighter in color and gentler in flavor. Many towns have their own brewery, where beer is produced.

keep their forks and their knives in those hands all the time. They do not put down their knife and use the fork in their right as we do. They use the blade of their knife to push food against their fork. Try this yourself. Does it feel awkward?

When drinking wine or beer after a meal, Germans usually toast each other. They raise their glass or mug and say "zum Wohl!", which means "to your health." Another popular toast is "prost," which means "cheers."

*Germans in Bavarian costumes enjoy drinking beer during Munich's famous Oktoberfest.*

**R E V I E W**

**Directions:**
Number your paper from 1 to 5. Answer the following questions.
1. What is the basic money unit of West Germany? What is the basic money unit of East Germany?
2. What is a youth hostel?
3. What is the German word for soccer?
4. How would you describe Bavaria's national costume?
5. What two American foods came directly from Germany?

# EAST AND WEST GERMANY

## MAP SKILLS

# LATITUDE AND LONGITUDE

Latitude marks go around the Earth in lines that are parallel to the equator. Longitude marks are parallel to a line that runs from the North Pole to the South Pole.

**Directions:** Use the map above to help you answer these questions about longitude and latitude.

1. (Munich, Hamburg) is near 48° north latitude.

2. (Hamburg, Cologne) is near 10° east longitude.

3. A city near 53° north latitude and 10° east longitude is (Stuttgart, Hannover).

4. (Berlin, Hamburg) is near 53° north latitude and 13° east longitude.

5. Dusseldorf, Cologne, and Bonn are near (7°, 25°) east longitude.

6. Frankfurt is near (8°, 50°) north latitude.

# CHAPTER 6 REVIEW

## Summary of Germany

*East and West Germany share a common culture that is the product of many years of history as a strong military power in Europe. United under the Holy Roman Empire and the might of Prussia, this central European nation has also controlled the cultures of other lands they have invaded.*

*A divided Germany was formed after World War II, and the defeat of Adolf Hitler's Third Reich. Today, West Germany is more closely aligned with the non-Communist nations of Western Europe. East Germany remains a strong ally of the Soviet Union, and has a Communist form of government. Despite this division, all Germans speak the same language. Most share in the same Christian religion.*

*Culture in modern Germany draws from the countries' past. It includes a love of outdoor sports, regional costumes worn on special occasions, and foods that were first prepared when modern-day refrigeration was not available.*

## Critical Thinking Skills

**Directions:** Give some serious thought to the questions below. Be sure to answer in complete sentences.

1. How has the lack of natural borders shaped German culture?
2. How would German culture be different today if Germany had a colder, more severe climate?
3. Who do you feel was more important to the development of German culture: Otto I or Adolf Hitler?
4. What kind of solution would you propose to reunite East and West Germany?
5. Do you think you would enjoy a visit to Germany? What are the reasons for your decision?

6. How did tribes from Germany change the course of European culture?
7. Which would you prefer: living in East Germany or living in West Germany?

## For Discussion

**Directions:** Discuss these questions with your class. Appoint one member of the class to write the ideas you discover on the board.

1. Compare the climate and geography of West and East Germany with the climate and geography of Italy.
2. What characteristics might Charlemagne have had that made him such a great leader?
3. Do you feel it is important for the government to support a public education system for its children, as Germany does?
4. Recently, people have been leaving Communist East Germany illegally and moving to Western, non-Communist countries. What are some of the reasons they might want to do this?

## Write It!

**Directions:** The Grimm Brothers lived in Germany during the 1700s. They traveled through their country collecting folk tales from every region. Some of these tales included *Snow White and the Seven Dwarfs* and *Little Red Riding Hood*. Retell one of these stories in your own words.

## For You to Do

**Directions:** Find a record or cassette that has a recording of Beethoven's Fifth Symphony. Play it for your class. As you listen to the record, write down the way you feel as you hear the music.

# POLAND

- Poland is in the center of Europe.
- It is surrounded on three sides by land.
- Poland's northern border is formed by the Baltic Sea.
- The capital of the Polish People's Republic is Warsaw.
- It is a Communist country with strong political ties to the Soviet Union.

## PART 1:
## Geography and Climate of Poland

In some cases, the natural boundaries of a nation have been determined by geography. Mountains or oceans isolate the country and protect it from invaders.

This is not the case with Poland. Poland has only one major mountain chain that lies between it and Czechoslovakia. This is the only natural land border that protects Poland. The Baltic Sea forms Poland's northern border. Most of the country is very flat. It is part of the Great European Plain. In the east, the land looks just like that of its neighbor, the Soviet Union. The land in the west resembles that of its other neighbor, East Germany.

Poland has no natural protection on these two borders. Many nations have easily invaded Poland, changing its history and culture.

**Map Study:** *Maps are drawn in a specific way. North is at the top of the map, south is at the bottom, east is on the right, and west is on the left. In what direction would you travel to go from East Germany to Poland? from Czechoslovakia to the Baltic Sea? from the U.S.S.R. (Russia) to Poland? from Krakow to Gdansk? from the Baltic Sea to Lodz?*

## Poland Has a Varied Climate

Poland has many different climate areas. The climate on the coastline is usually milder than the climate in other areas of the country. The climate in the mountains is usually much colder than the climate in the central plain.

However, in general, Poland has a *temperate* climate. This means that it is neither too hot nor too cold. Temperatures range from an average of 26° Fahrenheit in January, to 73° Fahrenheit in July.

Summers in Poland are never very hot. But in winter, most Poles can expect heavy snowfalls, particularly in Poland's mountainous regions.

Rainfall in this country is moderate. Poland gets an average of 24 inches of rain throughout the year.

Both these conditions are good for Poland's farmers. Crops grow well in this temperate climate.

## The Polish People's Republic Has Seven Land Areas

The geography of Poland is varied. It starts at the coastline of the Baltic Sea in the north and ends in the mountains that divide Poland and Czechoslovakia.

Poland has seven basic land areas. They range from the coastal lowlands in the north to the Western Carpathian and Sudetes Mountains in the south.

**R E V I E W**

**Directions:**
Number your paper from 1 to 4. Answer the following questions.
1. Poland has only one natural land border. How has this affected Polish history and culture?
2. Name the two mountain ranges in the southern part of Poland.
3. How would you describe Poland's climate?
4. Why is Poland's climate good for agriculture?

# PART 2:
## History of Poland

Historians think that *Slavic* people have lived in the country we now call Poland since 2000 B.C. Archaeologists have found that Poland is part of the oldest continuously inhabited region in Europe.

The Slavs lived in *clans*. The clans were very independent. However, after a time, one group became the strongest. This group was called the *Polane*. Their name means "people who live on a flat plain." Today, the country still has their name.

### Poland and Lithuania Unite

The early Poles needed help to overcome the *Tartars*. These Asian tribes swept into their country from the East, killing many Poles. Help for Poland came from a neighboring country, Lithuania. The Lithuanians joined the Poles in their fight against the invaders. Together, they defeated the Tartars.

The closeness of Poland and Lithuania continued for a long time. They stood together against all enemies. Later, members of the royal families of Poland and Lithuania married. Their descendants ruled the united countries for many years.

*The decorations inside of this Polish cottage are very bright and colorful. Poles have lived in small houses like these for hundreds of years.*

## Casimir the Great Brings a Strong Government to Poland

Poland had driven its enemies out of its borders. A great king was chosen to lead the country. His name was Casimir. He ruled Poland from 1333 to 1370.

Casimir brought peace to his country. He also increased its territory through skillful negotiations and diplomacy. The Polish economy bloomed under Casimir. So did its education system. Casimir himself founded the University of Krakow. This university is one of the oldest in Europe. He also welcomed many Jews into Poland. At the time, many other countries had forced all their Jewish citizens to leave.

*The Palace on the Water, the home of King Stanislaus Augustus Poniatowski, was considered to be one of the most beautiful 18th century residences in Europe. The palace now serves as a cultural center in the middle of Warsaw's Lazienki Park.*

## Poland Adopts a National Constitution

In 1505, Poland adopted its first national constitution. In this constitution, the government of the country was controlled by a group called the *Sejm*. The Sejm was a lawmaking group made up of Poland's nobles. This was the first time Poland had representative government on a national scale.

In 1572, the Polish ruler died. The new constitution said the Sejm had the right to elect Poland's king. They began this practice by choosing French Prince Henry of Valois. Henry became Henry I of Poland. He hated his job so much that he soon disguised himself and ran away. Henry I was certainly one of Poland's worst kings!

## Poland is Partitioned

The Polish nobles began to quarrel among themselves. Each wanted more power than the other. The Polish constitution also said that all laws had to be approved by every member of the Sejm. Some nobles refused to approve taxes. Without taxes, the country had no money to support an army or run its affairs. Poland's strong central government began to crumble.

Soon, other problems arose. People in the Ukrainian region of the Polish Empire rebelled. They won their independence from Poland in 1648. In 1655, Sweden took control of most of the provinces that surrounded the Baltic Sea. Turkey invaded Poland. The Polish were able to push them back to their own country, but only with great effort.

These trends continued into the 1700s. Poland's neighbors began to look greedily at the declining nation. Prussia on the west and Russia on the east were particularly interested in the Polish territories. They wanted Poland's land, its natural resources, and its ports on the Baltic Sea.

Russia, Prussia, and Austria-Hungary started absorbing Polish territory in 1772. In all, there were three *partitions*. By 1795, these countries had annexed all the Polish territory. Poland as a country no longer existed.

Polish people everywhere fought to keep the spirit of their country alive. Their efforts ensured that their culture did not die along with their country.

## Poland Starts on the Road to Freedom

The Poles continued to fight against the people who held their

---

### Pan Tadeusz

Many people think *Pan Tadeusz* is the greatest Polish poem ever written. It was authored by a Pole who was forced to leave his country after it was partitioned. His name was Adam Mickiewicz.

Mickiewicz went to France. He began to teach at a Paris university. But he missed Poland terribly. To comfort himself and other Poles who were in exile, he wrote his epic poem. Its name in English means "Sir Thaddeus."

Mickiewicz wrote of the Poland he left. He told of the traditions of the Polish culture he knew. The people in *Pan Tadeusz* were the people he knew in Poland. Mickiewicz did not want the Polish culture to die. He wanted Poles everywhere to work to bring their country back.

---

land. Several uprisings occurred. None were ever successful. The Poles did have some support from other people in Europe, including the French leader Napoleon.

World War I raged through Europe. American President Woodrow Wilson wanted to see an end to war. He drew up a plan, called the *Fourteen Points*, which he felt would bring peace. One point of Wilson's plan stated that Poland should be free.

The Polish welcomed this support. They had been fighting against the Russians, and were finally able to drive them out of Polish territory. In

# SPOTLIGHT
## S T O R Y

## The Broken Note

There is a church in Krakow that is very dear to all Poles. It has two names: the Church of Our Lady, or Panna Marja, and the Church of the Trumpeter.

Every hour, a trumpeter goes to the church's tower. He plays a short tune that always ends abruptly. The song he plays is called the Heynal. This means "the hymn of the broken note."

Each trumpeter is carrying on a centuries' old tradition. There was a young trumpeter at the church more than 700 years ago. As he looked down on the city, he saw great armies of Tartars invading Krakow. He tried to sound an alarm to warn the people. The young trumpeter continued to sound his alarm, even though Tartars had overrun the city. Suddenly, he was hit by a Tartar arrow. Still, he kept on playing. He tried to finish his song, but died before he could. His last note broke off.

Today, the trumpeter at the church in Krakow continues to sound this alarm every hour. He plays the short song four times, once for each direction of the compass. Poles everywhere consider the Heynal to be a sacred song. It is a symbol of their belief in their country and their culture. To most Poles it means that nothing, not even death, will stop them from protecting their country.

**Stop and Review**

Answer the following questions.
1. In what city is the Church of the Trumpeter located?
2. What is the name of the song that the trumpeter in the church's tower plays?
3. Why did a young trumpeter try to sound an alarm from the church tower more than 700 years ago?
4. Why does the Heynal always end abruptly?
5. Why do Poles consider the Heynal to be a sacred song? What does it symbolize for them?

*The tune of the broken note is still played at the Church of Our Lady in Krakow.*

1918, the Polish people proclaimed that their country was, once again, an independent republic.

## The Treaty of Versailles Reestablishes Poland

World War I ended in 1918. The following year, the *Treaty of Versailles* was signed. The treaty gave Poland a large amount of land that had been held by Prussia. (Today, Prussia is known as Germany.) This included most of the land around the Baltic Sea. But the port of Gdansk was placed under international control. It was called the free city of Danzig.

The treaty also set up a border between Poland and Germany. The Polish border with Russia was established by another treaty in 1921.

## Poland Tries to Rebuild

Poland had solved many of its problems, but quite a few lay ahead. The new country was in desperate need of a good school system and a strong government. The three parts of Poland had been apart for over 100 years. Poland's economy was in shambles. Now, the government had to see that all the people worked together toward common goals.

The new Polish constitution set up a democratic government. Others had different ideas about the way Poland should be run. One was Josef Pilsudski. Pilsudski first led the newly formed republic of Poland in 1918. After five years, he retired from politics. In 1926, he was back in the spotlight. Pilsudski led the Polish military in overthrowing the government. He then took over and ruled as a *dictator*.

## Poland's Freedom Ends

Poland's new freedom lasted only 20 years. In September 1939, Germany attacked Poland. Britain and France declared war on Germany. Two weeks later, Russia invaded

*The monument at Westerplatte marks the place where the first shots of World War II were fired.*

Poland. The Poles were defeated within a month. Germany and Russia carried out their secret plans and divided Polish lands between them.

### Poland Turns to Russia for Help

During World War II, over 6 million Poles were killed. This included almost 3 million Polish Jews. Many of them were killed in the concentration camps set up in Poland by the Germans.

Some Poles managed to escape to other countries. Germany and Russia were no longer allies. Many Poles felt that Russia was now their friend. After 1941, many of them moved to Russia. They believed that they had an ally in their fight against Hitler. Many of these people were Polish Communists. In 1942, they set up the Polish Worker's Party. This organization later became the basis for a new government in Poland. In 1944, Russia invaded Poland and started to drive out the Germans. The Russians recognized communism as the true government of Poland.

Polish Communists eventually took over the entire Polish government. However, Russia continued to influence them. The Russians had adopted a Communist government many years before. The Russian Communist Party placed Russians in important positions in the Polish government. In 1952, the Poles adopted a new constitution, based on the principles of Russia's constitution. The Polish government took control of all industries. Farmers were forced to give up their land and work on collective farms.

In one form or another, the Communist government continues to lead Poland today.

### Poland Today

Many Poles do not accept all the beliefs of a Communist state. Since the 1960s, there have been many strikes in Poland. People are upset about the limits communism places on their lives. Some also feel that Communist control has led to higher prices and food shortages.

*President Bush talks to Solidarity leader Lech Walesa (right) with the help of an interpreter.*

One group in particular has been at the front of these protests. It is an organization of free trade unions, led by Lech Walesa, called *Solidarity*, or *Solidarnösc* in Polish. This group won government recognition in 1989.

For the first time ever, members of Solidarity have been elected to many political positions, including that of prime minister. This is the first time that someone who is not a Communist has held this position.

R
E
V
I
E
W

**Directions:**
Number your paper from 1 to 5. Answer the following questions.
1. Who were the Polane?
2. What three countries annexed parts of Poland in the 1770s? What effect did these partitions have?
3. How did President Woodrow Wilson's ideas help Poland become a free country once again?
4. What happened to Poland during World War II?
5. What is Solidarity? How has Solidarity changed Poland's government?

# PART 3:
## Language and the Arts

The official language of Poland is Polish. It is a *Slavic* language. It was introduced into this area by the Slavic clans that settled here. The Czech and Russian languages are also part of the Slavic family of languages.

At first, each Slavic clan spoke its own language. However, the Polane soon became the leading tribe in Poland. Most other tribes adopted the language of the Polane.

Today, the word "slovo" means a written or painted character or word in most Slavic languages. In earlier days, Slavs used to call all people who spoke the same language "sloviane."

**The Polish Language**

The Polish alphabet is the same one that is used in English. It was brought to Poland by Christian monks in the 900s. Before that, people did not write in Polish.

The Poles have added nine special letters to their alphabet. These nine extra letters have special marks.

---

## Nine Extra Letters of the Polish Alphabet

| | | |
|---|---|---|
| Ąą | Ćć | Ęę |
| Łł | Ńń | Óó |
| Śś | Źź | Żż |

---

*These extra letters have special sounds. For example, Ś has a "Sh" sound.*

### Family Names in Poland

Some Polish names have the same endings. The most common ones are *-ski* and *-wicz* (pronounced "vich"). Some other common endings are *-ak* and *-czyk* (pronounced "chick"). These endings mean "of" and "related to." For example, in Polish, the word for beech tree is "buk." If someone's family name is Bukowski, it actually means "of the beech tree." However, like all names everywhere, these original meanings are often not very important.

In Poland, the women in a family have a slightly different name than the men. This is because they use a special form of the family name that is just for females. Their names use a feminine ending. The mother of the Bukowski family would write her name "Bukowska." *-Ska* is the feminine ending that matches *-ski*.

The most common family name in Poland is Kowalski. This means "of the forge." Do you know anyone whose family name is Polish?

---

### What's in a Name?

The Poles call their country Polska Rzeczypospolita Lodowa. In English, these words mean The Polish People's Republic. Their capital is not Warsaw; to the Poles, it is Warszawa.

Throughout the centuries, Poland has been held by other nations that brought their own culture and language with them. For example, Germany invaded and controlled Poland during World War II. The Germans set up concentration camps, where many Poles were slaughtered. The Poles do not want anyone to refer to any area in their country by its German name. In fact, it is against the law for anyone to enter Poland carrying a map that has German words on it. The Poles do not want their country to be associated with the Nazis and their reign of terror.

---

## Some Polish Words

| English | Polish | Pronunciation |
|---|---|---|
| Good morning | Dzien dobry | Dgen do´-bree |
| Thank you | Dziekuje | Dgen´-koo-jeh |
| Excuse me | Przepraszam | Pshe-pra´-sham |
| I don't speak Polish | Ja nie mówie po polsku | Ya nyeh moov´-yeh po pol´-skoo |

### Learning How to Speak Polish Can Be Difficult for Americans

Many Americans find it hard to learn how to speak Polish. This is because Polish has so many words that are nothing like words in American English.

Just to get a flavor of the language, look at the words in the box above. You can see how they are pronounced. Try saying them out loud.

### Polish Literature

Polish literature really grew during the *Renaissance.* This was a time in Europe when there was a renewed interest in learning and the arts. Some of the first Polish writers were poets. They included Mikolaj Rej and Jan Kochanowski. Many people call this time the Golden Age of Polish literature.

### Polish Literature Keeps the Spirit of the Country Alive

The Polish nation was partitioned among its three neighbors at the end of the 1700s. Poland's authors now had a greater responsibility. They and other artists had to keep the culture of their country alive. In their

*Statue of Adam Mickiewicz, the author of* Pan Tadeusz

own way, they urged their country-men not to give up on Poland.

Some Polish authors did stay in Polish territory during the partitions. One of these was Henryk Sienkiewicz. His most famous novel was called *Quo Vadis?* In 1905, Sienkiewicz was given the Nobel Prize for literature. This international prize has been awarded to the world's best writers.

However, many other writers left Poland during this time. One of these was Adam Mickiewicz, the poet who wrote *Pan Tadeusz.* Another writer was Jozef Korzeniowski. When he left Poland, this author changed his name to Joseph Conrad. Readers around the world still enjoy his works, including *Lord Jim* and *Heart of Darkness.*

Another famous author who left Poland in the 1900s is Isaac Bashevis Singer. His stories tell about Jewish life in Poland. Singer was also awarded a Nobel Prize for his work.

## Polish Music Comes From Mixed Roots

Polish music is an interesting blend. Some music comes from the traditions of the farmers and workers in the country. Other music comes from the people who were part of Poland's noble class.

For example, the *polka* is a very popular Polish dance. Remember that the name for Poland in Polish is "Polska." "Polka" is another form of this Polish word. The polka is a lively dance. Many Poles in rural areas love to dance the polka. Polkas are often played by a band that features an accordion.

The national dance of Poland is called the *mazurka.* It is a complex dance that started in Poland's rural areas.

However, the Poles also have a stately folk dance called the *polonaise.* This dance was part of the life of every Polish noble person. Frederic

*The Chopin Monument in Warsaw*

Chopin, the famous Polish composer, has written many beautiful polonaises.

Chopin was a Pole who lived in exile outside his country during the time of the partitions. He worked hard to keep the musical tradition of Poland alive. Many of his works are based on traditional Polish folk songs and dances. Chopin's Funeral March has been used to mark sad occasions all over the world. Some have said that Chopin meant it only for his beloved Poland.

---

**R E V I E W**

**Directions:**
Number your paper from 1 to 4. Answer the following questions.
1. Name two languages that are part of the Slavic family of languages.
2. How did the Polish people change the alphabet that they adopted from the English?
3. Name one of the Polish writers who were part of Poland's Golden Age of literature.
4. What is the national dance of Poland?

---

# PART 4:
## Life in Modern Poland

Poland's basic money unit is called the *zloty*. In 1989, it was worth about one-eighteenth of a penny.

Before World War II, most Poles were subsistence farmers. They usually grew just enough crops for themselves to eat. Today, it is a different story.

After the war, Poland developed its industry. Poland is now one of the leading industrial countries in Eastern Europe. Only the Soviet Union produces more goods than Poland. At least a third of all Polish workers have jobs in industry. The wages these workers receive are not very high. Consumer goods are expensive. It takes the average worker two days' salary to buy a pair of shoes. A suit requires two weeks' salary. To buy a car, a Polish worker would have to spend all the money he or she could earn in six years.

In almost all Communist countries, the government owns and manages most industries. Over 90 percent of the industries in Poland are owned by the government.

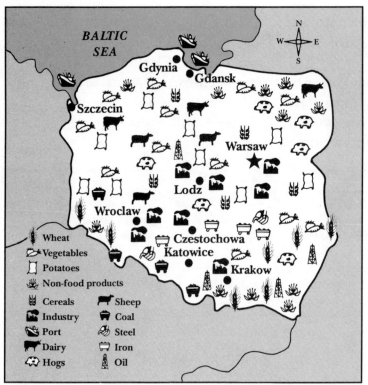

BALTIC SEA

Gdynia
Gdansk
Szczecin
Warsaw
Lodz
Wroclaw
Czestochowa
Katowice
Krakow

Wheat
Vegetables
Potatoes
Non-food products
Cereals
Industry
Port
Dairy
Hogs
Sheep
Coal
Steel
Iron
Oil

**Map Study:** *What are two of Poland's major ports? Is most of Poland's industrial activity located in the north or south? Name two kinds of economic activity that take place just west of Katowice. Name two agricultural products grown near Poland's Baltic Sea coast. Name two cities where industrial activity takes place.*

## Education

During the Middle Ages, Poland was a great center of learning. Universities throughout the country attracted many bright students. One of these students was Mikolaj Kopernik. We know him today as Nicholas Copernicus. Copernicus was the first person to discover that the sun was the center of the universe. His work paved the way for many others, including Johan Kepler and Sir Isaac Newton.

Today, Poles still have a great respect for education. About 98 percent of the population can read and write. Each Polish child has to attend school from ages seven to fifteen. The government pays for all of this education. Students first go to elementary schools. After that, they can attend a vocational school or a high school. Any Polish student who wishes to continue his or her studies at a university must pass a special test.

Students in Poland study most of the same subjects that you do, such as mathematics, science, and history. In addition, they must study the Russian language. Many students also study French and German.

## Religion

Poles are very loyal to their faith. Almost 95 percent of them are

## The Nesting Dolls

If you look in a Warsaw kindergarten, you might find an intriguing toy. It is a set of nesting dolls. Each doll is smaller than the next. Each fits neatly into the other. This toy looks like it is only one doll, but this is not so.

Storytellers throughout Poland use these dolls to tell many of the stories that are part of their folklore. They open up the dolls to reveal each smaller one. As they do this, they say, "My great grandmother told this story to my grandmother. My grandmother told the story to my mother. My mother told it to me. And now I am telling it to you."

Although these toys were not invented in Poland, the Polish people have made them their own. Some people say this is because many Slavic people have a great love of folklore. One character in their folklore is Marzanna. Marzanna is a very old grandmother. She also represents death. At the end of winter, children would build a straw figure of Marzanna. Then they would burn her, or throw her in the river. Before they did this, they would take out a small doll hidden inside the Marzanna. They would bring the small doll back to their village. In effect, they had killed winter and brought back spring.

*Polish nesting dolls*

*Pope John Paul II has urged the Polish government to allow its people more freedom.*

baptized Roman Catholics. About 90 percent of them attend church services every Sunday. This is very unusual for a Communist country.

The Communist Party tried to discourage Polish people from attending church during the 1940s and 1950s. They wanted to eliminate the Church's influence. They were not successful. Poles thought the government was trying to take away too much of their freedom and rebelled. The Communist Party stopped trying to undermine the Church.

# POLAND

Today, the entire Roman Catholic Church is led by a Pole. His name is Karol Cardinal Wojtyla. In 1978, the Church chose him to be Pope. He took a new name, Pope John Paul II. Pope John Paul is the first Polish Pope. He is also the first Pope chosen from a Communist country, and the first non-Italian Pope since 1523.

## Entertainment

Polish people today have many opportunities to enjoy themselves. Their *standard of living* is one of the highest among Communist countries. However, it is not as high as the standard of living in the countries in Western Europe. A standard of living describes the general economic well-being of people in a country. It includes measures of their income and buying power.

*Ballet and opera have a loyal following in Poland. Above is a scene from a ballet performance at the Wielki Opera and Ballet Theatre.*

One universal form of entertainment is television. Television sets are a luxury in Poland. Only half of all Polish homes have one. The government owns two national networks that broadcast programs to homes all across the country.

Poles enjoy many other forms of entertainment. Attending the circus is a favorite activity. The Warsaw Circus, or *Cyrk*, is famous all over the world. Others like to attend the ballet or opera. There, they enjoy the work of many modern Polish composers. These artists have used the cultural traditions of their country as themes for their work. Poles also take great interest in movies.

The Polish people love to explore their country. Hiking and camping

*Like people everywhere, the Poles enjoy outdoor activities such as sailing on the Baltic.*

are popular in this beautiful country. As do most Europeans, many Poles enjoy playing soccer.

## Celebrations

Poles have had their farms and their religion when everything else was gone, including their country. Their land and their faith have held them together. These things not only play a big part in daily life, but in special celebrations as well.

In late August, people throughout Poland celebrate the harvest. They give thanks for their bounty and say special prayers giving thanks to God for their crops. This festival is somewhat like the Thanksgiving your family celebrates.

But the biggest celebrations of the year are centered on religious events. These are the two biggest holidays of the Christian year — Christmas and Easter.

## Christmas

Like all Polish holidays, Christmas is a time for the family. All members of the family join together to celebrate. Many homes have a Christmas tree. Singing carols and enjoying special meals are all a part of this holiday. Is this similar to the way your family celebrates this holiday season?

*The Feast of the Wine Harvest in Zielona Góra, Poland*

Most traditions of this holiday in Poland center on Christmas Eve. On that night, the family dinner table may be covered with straw. This is to remind the family that Christ was born in a stable. An extra place is always set at the table. This place may be taken by an unexpected guest. But, traditionally, it is set for the Christ Child.

Before everyone eats, each person gives a special wafer to the others at the table. The wafer is called an *oplatek*. As they give the wafer, each person asks the other to forgive them for things that they did wrong during the year.

The Christmas celebration lasts until January 6. This is Epiphany.

The church celebrates this as the time the Three Kings found the baby Jesus. In the streets, children can enjoy many puppet shows about the birth of Christ. Each town has a special pageant. On Epiphany, people give each other small gifts.

## Easter

Easter is also a time for the family to visit their friends. On Easter Sunday, most Poles will visit their neighbors to celebrate. They take the food they will eat to a local church on the Saturday before Easter. There, the priests will bless it. This ceremony is called Swieconka. Traditionally, the Poles serve breads, sausages, and colored eggs as they enjoy this day.

## Polish Foods Reflect the Culture

People in Poland often eat foods that have been prepared by Poles for many generations. These include rye and wheat grains, potatoes, and cabbage. These foods are still the basis of the Polish diet. In earlier times, these products were easily grown on their small farms. Cabbage was their main source of vitamin C. Until recently, Poles could not buy many citrus fruits. Citrus fruits are a very good source of vitamin C.

The Polish word for vegetables is *wloszcyzna*. It means "Italian things." Some vegetables were first introduced by a Polish queen who came from Italy.

Polish people do eat meat, but they do not eat as much of it as Americans do. Sometimes, this is because of shortages in the government-controlled stores. Often, it is simply a matter of choice. People who live on the coast enjoy all kinds of seafood. People living in the mountains eat foods that are easily found near their homes, including wild mushrooms.

## Meal Times

If you were to visit a Polish family, they would probably serve you a very light breakfast. Rolls, butter, jam, and tea are typically a part of this breakfast.

Around 10:00 a.m., Poles usually stop working to have a sandwich. You would probably appreciate this snack, because the main meal does not come until late in the day. After work is over, around 3:00 or 4:00 in the afternoon, you would enjoy the main meal of the day with them. This is when you would have the chance to sample some of their national dishes. Your first course might include a beet soup with vegetables and sour cream called barszcz. After that, your hosts might serve golabki, or stuffed cabbage rolls. Other main courses that Poles enjoy serving include zajac (rabbit in sour cream), kaczka (wild duck with apples), or bryndza (sheep's milk with cheese and chives). The Polish are also known for their kielbasa (sausage), and kolduny (beef turnovers). Which of these Polish specialties would you prefer to eat?

You and your Polish hosts would probably not eat dinner until 8:00 or 9:00 in the evening. Their dinner is a light meal, similar to our lunch.

**REVIEW**

**Directions:**
Number your paper from 1 to 5. Answer the following questions.
1. What is the basic money unit in Poland?
2. How would you define standard of living?
3. What are some of the traditional Polish Christmas customs?
4. Name the three foods that are the basis of the Polish diet.
5. Why do the Poles call vegetables "Italian things"?

# MAP SKILLS

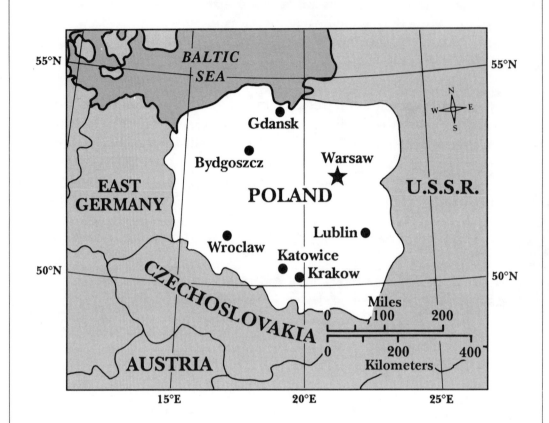

## SCALE

A scale on a map gives the measurement on the map that represents actual distance. The scale for this map shows that one-and-a-quarter inches equals 200 miles. The scale also tells us that three-quarters of an inch equals 200 kilometers.

**Directions:**

Using the map and its scale on this page, answer these questions about Poland.

1. The distance from the eastern to the western border of Poland is about (150, 400) miles.

2. The distance from the northern to the southern border of Poland is about (200, 375) miles.

3. It is about (50, 170) miles from Warsaw to Gdansk.

4. It is about (200, 10) miles from Warsaw to Wroclaw.

5. Krakow is about (75, 300) miles south of Gdansk.

6. The Baltic coastline of Poland is over (600, 200) miles long.

7. It is about (300, 100) miles from Gdansk to Bydgoszcz.

# CHAPTER 7 REVIEW

## Summary of Poland

The culture in the nation of Poland has developed over many years, but is based on the early Slavic cultures of the people who first lived in the area. The traditions of this early culture, shared with the effects of a varied geography and climate, and a long history of conflict, still color Polish life today.

Poland moved from its early position of power to a state where the nation of Poland did not even exist. Poles depended on the traditions of their shared culture to unify them after the partitions. Today, this same cultural unity is bringing this nation a renewed sense of its independence. Modern-day Poland was formed as a Communist nation after World War II. Today, the free trade union Solidarity has emerged to lead the nation toward a more diversified government.

The Poles share a common language, and a rich history of contributions to the arts and sciences. Like most Europeans, the majority of Poles can read and write. This enables them to enjoy many of the great works of literature Polish authors have created. Poles still continue to celebrate such feasts as Easter and Christmas, which are rich in the traditions of their culture.

## Critical Thinking Skills

**Directions:** Give some serious thought to the questions below. Be sure to answer in complete sentences.

1. Poland has only one natural land boundary. How has this affected the culture?
2. Do you feel it is a good idea for the noble people to elect a country's king? Why do you feel this way?
3. If you were a Polish person after the partitions, what would you have done to bring your country back together?

4. Discuss some of the things that made it possible for Poland to reestablish itself as a country.
5. What effect has Communism had on Poland's culture?

## For Discussion

**Directions:** Discuss these questions with your class. Appoint one class member to write the ideas you discover on the board.

1. Do you agree with Woodrow Wilson's idea that each nation should have a right to have its own government? Can there ever be a case where this is not true?
2. Polish leaders are struggling today to establish a government that is more representative of the goals of the people. In the end, do you feel Poland will remain a Communist nation, or change its government to one that is more like those in Western Europe?
3. Like most Europeans, Poles do not eat as much beef as do Americans. What does this say about their culture?

## Write It!

**Directions:** Your grandmother is planning to visit Poland. You have just returned from a visit there. Write a list of the special things your grandmother should know about Poland to make her trip more enjoyable.

## For You to Do

**Directions:** As a class, arrange for a teacher to visit your class to teach you how to do the polka. Records of polka music are available from your school or local library. Once your class has learned the basics of the dance, invite another class to visit and learn the polka.

# GLOSSARY

**acropolis**—in ancient Greece, the high hill in each city-state around which the city built a wall of rocks; literally "high city"

**Allies**—a group of nations including France, Great Britain, Russia, and the United States that joined together in the defense of Europe during World Wars I and II

**alphabet**—the letters used by a particular language

**Angle-land**—Great Britain's name during the 400s

**Angles**—a German tribe that invaded England around the year 400

**archaeologists**—scientists who study the material remains of past civilizations

**armistice**—an agreement to stop fighting during a war

**Attic**—the language of Athens in ancient times; a dialect of Greek

**Bastille**—the French prison that was captured at the beginning of the French Revolution

**Bavarian Alps**—the mountains that form the southern border of Germany in the region of Bavaria; part of the largest mountain system in Europe

**Blackshirts**—a political group started in Italy by Benito Mussolini; the group served as a secret police organization

**bouzouki**—a Greek musical instrument that resembles a mandolin

**Breton**—a Celtic dialect spoken by French people living in the region of Brittany on the Atlantic coast of France

**calcio**—the Italian name for soccer

**Celts**—a warlike tribe of people that settled in many parts of Europe and were conquered by the Romans

**centime**—in France, a unit of money that equals one-hundredth of a franc

**city-states**—small geographic areas that became independent powers in ancient Greece

**clan**—a loosely unified group of people usually composed of members of an extended family

**cockney**—a dialect of English spoken by people who live in the East End of London

**common law**—the principles of law established in England under King Alfred the Great

**Communist**—a kind of government, or a person who believes in a type of government, in which the central government controls all means of producing goods

**confederation**—a loose union of separate states or nations

**Consilium Plebis**—in ancient Rome, a lawmaking group that represented the people

**constitution**—the document used by different countries to establish the form and rules of their central government

**continent**—a large land division on the Earth

**cricket**—a game sometimes described as the national sport of the United Kingdom

**culture**—the way of life followed by a group of people including their beliefs, customs, inventions, language, technology, and traditions

**Cyrk**—the world-famous Warsaw circus

**Danelaw**—the name of an area in northern England controlled by the Danes in the 800s

**Dark Ages**—a period of time in European history that began with the fall of the Roman Empire in 476 and continued until the 900s

**David**—a famous statue sculpted by Michelangelo

**demotic**—the form of modern Greek that most Greeks speak today

**deutsche mark**—the basic money unit of East and West Germany

**dialect**—similar forms of the same language spoken by members of a culture who live in different regions

**dictator**—a person who has absolute control of a government

**dirndl skirt**—a full, colorful skirt with a wide waistband that is laced up; a traditional costume of the Bavarian region of Germany

**dowry**—a sum of money or property that the bride's family gives to the groom when they marry

**drachma**—the basic money unit of Greece

**duchy**—a separate region under the control of a duke

**Edict of Nantes**—a document signed by Henry IV, guaranteeing the French people freedom of religion

**empire**—a large amount of territory controlled by one country or person

**epic poem**—a form of verse that tells a story of the adventures or accomplishments of a people, or relates a heroic story from a culture's past

**equator**—an imaginary line that circles the Earth at its middle

**European Economic Community**—a loose union of European countries set up to work toward the economic well-being of each member

**fascism**—a type of government in which the central government has absolute control over industry and communications in the country

**fleet**—a large group of naval vessels

**Fourteen Points**—President Woodrow Wilson's plan to end World War I

**franc**—the basic money unit of France

**Franks**—the most powerful Germanic tribe that controlled France after the fall of the Roman Empire

**füssball**—the German word for soccer

**Gallia**—the most powerful Celtic tribe that inhabited France before the birth of Christ

**gondola**—the small boats that people use to travel around Venice, Italy

**Hanseatic League**—an important group of cities in Germany that united in the late 1200s and grew in power as the Holy Roman Empire lost its power

**Helladic civilization**—another name for the Mycenean culture; an ancient culture that developed on the mainland of Greece around the year 3000 B.C.

**Hellas**—another name for the Greek mainland

**Heptarchy**—in England, the system of seven loosely united kingdoms set up by the Angles and Saxons between the years 500 and 800

**High German**—called "Hochdeutsch" in German; a German dialect that is spoken in the southern, higher regions of Germany

**highlands**—geographic regions in the United Kingdom that include mountains, deep valleys, and plateaus

**hostels**—inns in many European nations that offer low-cost accommodations to traveling students

**Huguenots**—French people who belonged to the Protestant faith

**Hundred Years' War**—a conflict between France and England that began in 1337 and lasted 116 years

**Il Duce**—the name by which the Italian dictator Benito Mussolini was known; "the leader" in Italian

**illiterate**—unable to read or write

**Industrial Revolution**—a movement that began in Great Britain in the 19th century when people started using machines powered by water or steam to manufacture goods more quickly

**island**—a land form that is surrounded on all sides by water

**Jutes**—a Germanic tribe that invaded England around the year 400

**kafenion**—In Greece, local cafés or coffee houses that are usually located outdoors in a central part of town

**kaiser**—"emperor" in German; Wilhelm I became Kaiser of a unified Germany in 1871

**katharevousa**—the form of modern Greek that is used in most scientific books and by the Greek government

**kindergarten**—a "children's garden" in German; schools for pre-school children, first established in Germany

**koine**—a simplified form of the Attic language

**Latin**—the language of the Roman Empire

**le foot**—in French, the word for soccer

**league**—a group of regions or cities that unite for self-defense or other purposes

**lederhosen**—leather shorts with broad suspenders that are a traditional costume in the Bavarian region of Germany

**lepta**—a unit of Greek money; one hundred lepta equal one drachma

**liceo**—an Italian high school where pupils study arts and language

**lira**—the basic money unit of Italy; the plural form is lire

**loch**—the Scottish word for "lake"

**lough**—the word for "lake" that is used in Northern Ireland

**Low German:**—called "Plattdeutsch" in German; the dialect that is spoken in the northern, flatter parts of Germany

**lyric poem**—a short form of verse first used by the Greeks that relates the feelings of the writer

**Maginot Line**—a line of defenses the French built to protect their border with Germany

**Magna Carta**—a document signed by King John of England in 1215 that limited the power of the king and gave some power of governing to the noble classes

**mazurka**—the national dance of Poland

**Mediterranean climate**—the warm climate in several countries that adjoin the Mediterranean; caused by the flow of winds over the warm water

**Minoan culture**—an ancient Greek civilization that developed on the island of Crete around the year 3000 B.C.

**moors**—in the United Kingdom, areas of the highlands that have very poor soil

**Mycenaean culture**—an ancient Greek civilization that developed on the mainland of Greece around the year 3000 B.C.; also known as the Helladic civilization

**Nazis**—the National Socialist German Workers' Party, led by Adolf Hitler

**Nike**—a Greek word meaning "bringer of peace"

**Normans**—people from France who took over the throne of England in 1066, and then advanced to Ireland

**North Atlantic Current**—the warm ocean current that flows past the west coast of Ireland and the coast of Great Britain

**North Sea**—a part of the Atlantic Ocean that lies between Great Britain and mainland Europe

# GLOSSARY

**opera**—a type of play created in Italy that is sung instead of spoken

**oplatek**—a special wafer that is used during the Christmas season in Poland

**Papal States**—an area in central Italy that was controlled by the Roman Catholic Church from 756 to 1870

**Parliament**—in the United Kingdom and other countries, the legislative body of the government

**partition**—a process through which territory is divided; Poland lost all of its land through a series of partitions

**Pax Romana**—in ancient Rome, the period from 27 B.C. to 180 A.D., when no one challenged the power of the Roman Empire; literally, "Roman Peace"

**peninsula**—a land form that is surrounded on three sides by water

**philosophy**—the study of learning and thinking; a science invented by the Greeks

**plateau**—a land area that is raised above the surrounding land, but still has a relatively level surface

**Polane**—the clan that became the leader of the Slavic clans in Poland; its name means "people who live on a flat plain"

**polis**—the Greek word for city-states

**polka**—a popular Polish dance

**polonaise**—a stately dance of the noble class in Poland

**pound**—the basic money unit of the United Kingdom

**precipitation**—rain, snow, sleet, or hail

**province**—in ancient history, a specific land area controlled by the Roman Empire

**pubs**—in the United Kingdom, neighborhood gathering places where people go for entertainment; an abbreviated form of "public house"

**rationalism**—a philosophy of writing that emphasizes the reasons behind human actions

**Reformation**—a movement by many religious leaders in Europe that led to the development of several Protestant faiths; the Reformation began in 1517 in Germany

**Renaissance**—starting in the 1300s, the time in Europe when there was a rebirth of interest in learning and the arts

**reparations**—payments made after a war to compensate the countries that suffered damages

**republic**—a form of government in which the people elect the officials that make their laws; the government is led by an elected official as opposed to a monarch

**Romance languages**—languages that are based on the Latin language of the Roman Empire; includes Spanish, French, and Italian

**rural**—areas that are not part of the city and its surrounding suburbs; includes many farms and is generally a less populated region than urban areas

**Saxons**—Germanic tribes that invaded England around the year 400

**Sejm**—the lawmaking body in Poland

**Senate**—in ancient Rome, a group that advised the Emperor on decisions of government

**serfdom**—a practice by which noblemen would force peasants to be their slaves

**Slavic**—relating to the cultures of Poland, Czechoslovakia, Bulgaria, Yugoslavia, and Russia

**social scientists**—people who study societies and culture, including anthropologists, historians, archaeologists, sociologists, political scientists, and economists

**Socialist**—a form of government that advocates government ownership and control of industry

**Solidarity**—in Poland, an organization of free trade unions

**Standard German**—a form of German that is based on High German and is used today in schools, books, magazines, and in other forms of public communication

**standard of living**—a measure of the general economic well-being of people living in a nation

**Tartars**—a group of people from Asia who invaded Poland

**temperate**—a term used to describe a climate that is neither too hot nor too cold

**Third Reich**—the name Hitler gave to Germany under his leadership

**Tour de France**—the prestigious bicycle race held annually in France

**Treaty of Versailles**—the official treaty that ended World War I

**tuition**—fees paid by some families for their children to attend private schools

**Weimar Republic**—the weak government established in Germany after World War I

**wloszcyzna**—the Polish word for vegetables; it means "Italian things"

**volcano**—mountains or hills formed by the flow of melted rock that leaves the center of the Earth through vents; some volcanoes remain active

**zloty**—the basic unit of money in Poland

# INDEX